CALIFORNIA BUCKET LIST

Set Off on **120 Epic Adventures** and Discover
Incredible Destinations to Live Out Your Dreams
While Creating Unforgettable Memories
that Will Last a Lifetime.

**(Online Digital MAP included - access it through
the link provided in the MAP Chapter of this book)**

Becrepress Travel

CALIFORNIA BUCKET LIST

CALIFORNIA BUCKET LIST

TABLE OF CONTENTS

CALIFORNIA BUCKET LIST

CALIFORNIA BUCKET LIST

CALIFORNIA BUCKET LIST

CALIFORNIA BUCKET LIST

INTRODUCTION

Welcome to a journey that promises to be nothing short of spectacular—your ultimate guide to the sun-drenched, diverse, and dazzling state of California!

California Bucket List: Set Off on 120 Epic Adventures is your golden ticket to exploring the Golden State in all its glory. Imagine an adventure so grand it feels like stepping into a dream, where every sunrise brings a new marvel and every sunset wraps up a day of unforgettable experiences. That's the magic we're offering in this guide, packed with 120 of California's most breathtaking destinations!

Envision yourself standing at the edge of the Pacific Ocean, the salty breeze tousling your hair as you explore the stunning Carmel River State Beach, or feeling the thrill of Disney California Adventure Park's rides whisking you into a world of imagination and excitement.

Whether you're enchanted by the historic charm of Hearst Castle or the awe-inspiring grandeur of Yosemite Falls, this guide will transport you from the golden beaches of Santa Monica to the snow-capped peaks of the Sierra Nevada, and every spectacular stop in between. Each destination has been carefully curated not only for its beauty but for the adventures it offers.
You'll find detailed descriptions that bring these places to life, along with practical information to make your journey seamless.

We've included addresses so you never lose your way, nearby cities to give you context, and precise GPS coordinates for those who love to navigate with precision. Discover the best times to visit each spot, ensuring your trip is perfectly timed for ideal weather and fewer crowds. We've also outlined any tolls or access fees, so there are no surprises—just pure, exhilarating exploration.

Our Did You Know sections will surprise you with fascinating trivia, and we've even provided websites for each destination, so you can stay updated on the latest happenings and plan your visit to perfection. To make your adventure even smoother, you'll find an interactive state map with all the destinations pre-loaded. Say goodbye to the

CALIFORNIA BUCKET LIST

frustration of navigating outdated maps or fiddling with apps—this map is your personal guide to California's wonders.

So, are you ready to dive headfirst into the magic of California? Picture yourself marveling at the Golden Gate Bridge, enjoying the thrilling rides at Six Flags Magic Mountain, or soaking in the tranquil beauty of Muir Woods National Monument.

California Bucket List is not just a guide; it's a passport to creating memories that will last a lifetime. So grab your gear, pack your sense of wonder, and let's embark on an epic adventure through the Golden State. The sun-soaked beaches, majestic mountains, and vibrant cities of California are waiting for you—so let's get started!

ABOUT CALIFORNIA

To access the Digital Map, please refer to the 'Map Chapter' in this book

Landscape of California

California's landscape is a mesmerizing tapestry of natural wonders and dynamic terrains, crafted by nature's most dramatic artistry. From the sun-kissed beaches of Santa Monica to the rugged splendor of Yosemite Valley, the state is a land of incredible contrasts and breathtaking beauty.

Imagine starting your journey on the golden shores of Venice Beach, where the surf meets the vibrant boardwalk, and then venturing inland to the lush, ancient groves of Muir Woods National Monument. Here, towering redwoods, some more than 2,000 years old, create a cathedral of green that whispers tales of centuries past.

Travel south, and you'll find yourself at the awe-inspiring Badwater Basin, the lowest point in North America, where the stark, sun-baked salt flats stretch out beneath a vast, azure sky.

As you explore further, the dramatic landscapes of Death Valley and the mystical hues of Zabriskie Point offer a view of nature's raw, untamed beauty.
Transition from the desert's arid expanse to the lush, rolling hills of Point Lobos, where the Pacific Ocean crashes against rugged cliffs, and the diverse marine life thrives beneath the waves. California's coast is equally spellbinding, from the scenic 17-Mile Drive, which weaves through cypress-studded coastlines, to the charming Carmel River State Beach, where the gentle surf and sweeping sands invite relaxation and reflection.

Flora and Fauna of California

California's flora and fauna weave a spectacular tapestry of natural wonders that will ignite your imagination and spark your sense of adventure. Picture yourself amid the towering giants of Mariposa Grove, where the ancient sequoias rise like colossal pillars of nature, their immense trunks and canopies inspiring awe and reverence. These magnificent trees, some of the largest and oldest living beings on the planet, offer a glimpse into a world where time seems to stand still.

Journey into the tranquil embrace of Muir Woods National Monument, where coastal redwoods form a lush, green cathedral. Here, sunlight filters through the dense foliage, casting a magical glow that dances on the forest floor. The air is rich with the earthy scent of damp moss and ferns, creating a serene escape from the clamor of everyday life. Nearby, Point Lobos presents a striking contrast with its rugged coastal cliffs adorned with vibrant wildflowers. The sight of these delicate blooms swaying against the backdrop of a vast, azure ocean is nothing short of enchanting.

As you explore the arid expanses of Badwater Basin and Dante's View, the landscape transforms into a mesmerizing desert realm. Hardy sagebrush and resilient desert wildflowers add splashes of life and color to the sun-baked, salt-strewn flats. These plants have adapted to thrive in one of the harshest climates, showcasing nature's remarkable adaptability.

California's diverse ecosystems are also a haven for a myriad of wildlife. Witness the majestic black bears roaming through the ancient forests of Yosemite or watch the playful sea lions lounging on the rocky shores of La Jolla Cove. The state's commitment to conservation is evident in places like the San Diego Zoo Safari Park and The Living Desert Zoo and Gardens, where you can observe and learn about a wide range of exotic and native animals.

Whether you're exploring the meticulously cultivated beauty of the Japanese Tea Garden in Golden Gate Park or marveling at the unique flora of the Indian Canyons, California's natural heritage promises endless discovery and inspiration. Each destination invites you to experience and appreciate the rich, vibrant tapestry of life that defines the Golden State, making every visit a new adventure into nature's splendor.

Climate of California

California's climate is as diverse and captivating as its landscapes, offering a weather palette that ranges from sun-drenched beaches to crisp mountain air, and everything in between.
Picture this: you're lounging on the golden sands of Santa Monica State Beach, where the Pacific Ocean's gentle waves kiss your toes under the warm, endless sunshine. This is California's Mediterranean climate at its best, with mild, wet winters and hot, dry summers that create the perfect backdrop for beachside bliss.

But the Golden State's climate is not one-dimensional. Venture inland to the heart of California's deserts, and you'll find the striking extremes of Badwater Basin. As one of the hottest places on Earth, its blistering temperatures are tempered by breathtaking vistas of salt flats and rugged terrain. And yet, a mere few hours away, you can revel in the crisp, cool air of the Sierra Nevada, where the alpine climate of Yosemite National Park offers a refreshing contrast with its snow-capped peaks and lush meadows.

As you explore the vibrant cities of Los Angeles and San Francisco, you'll experience the microclimates that add character to each locale. In San Francisco, the iconic fog rolls in from the bay, creating a cool, misty charm that envelops landmarks like the Golden Gate Bridge and the bustling Fisherman's Wharf. Meanwhile, in the sun-drenched expanse of Palm Springs, you'll bask in the high desert heat, perfect for enjoying the oasis-like pools and striking mid-century architecture.

Throughout California, the climate is as varied as the adventures that await. Whether you're hiking through the lush groves of Muir Woods, exploring the vibrant urban landscapes of Downtown Disney District, or taking in the dramatic sunsets at Sunset Cliffs Natural Park, California's weather enhances every experience. It's a state where each region offers its own unique weather story, making it a place of endless exploration and discovery.

So pack your bags and get ready to embrace the sunny, cool, or even frosty delights that California has to offer!

History of California

California's history is a rich tapestry of cultures, explorers, pioneers, and dreams, stretching back thousands of years and transforming the Golden State into a vibrant mosaic of human endeavor and natural beauty. Imagine standing where ancient Native American tribes, such as the Chumash and Miwok, first tread upon these lands, their deep connection to the earth shaping the region's cultural heritage long before European explorers set sail.

The Age of Exploration began in the early 16th century when the intrepid Spanish explorer Juan Rodríguez Cabrillo first set foot on California's shores, landing at what is now Cabrillo National Monument. This moment marked the beginning of a dramatic and transformative period in California's history. As Spanish missions spread across the state, their influence is still palpable in the charming old-world ambiance of Old Town San Diego and the historic Mission San Juan Capistrano, where the echoes of early settlers' lives can be felt.

The California Gold Rush of 1849 ignited a frenzy of excitement and opportunity, drawing thousands of fortune seekers to the state. This period of rapid growth and transformation left an indelible mark on California's identity, shaping its economic and cultural landscape. Explore the vibrant history of this era at the California State Railroad Museum in Old Sacramento, where the steam engines that once chugged across the frontier now stand as symbols of innovation and perseverance.

As you delve into California's more recent history, the 20th century brings an explosion of creativity and innovation. Hollywood, with its iconic Hollywood Sign and the Hollywood Walk of Fame, became the global epicenter of film and entertainment, where legends were born and cinematic dreams were made.
Disneyland Park and Disney California Adventure Park embody the spirit of imagination and adventure that Walt Disney himself brought to life, making California the land where fairy tales and fun come to life.

But California's story doesn't end there. It's also a land of groundbreaking scientific discovery and technological advancement. The California Science Center in Los Angeles stands as a testament to the state's dedication to exploration and learning, reflecting the same pioneering spirit that led to the construction of the Golden Gate Bridge—a feat of engineering prowess that spans San Francisco Bay and symbolizes the bold vision of the state.

From the rugged landscapes of Yosemite National Park, where the awe-inspiring Glacier Point and the General Sherman Tree stand as natural monuments to the past, to the grandeur of Hearst Castle, built by media mogul William Randolph Hearst, California's history is a story of adventure, innovation, and relentless ambition.

Each destination offers a unique glimpse into the myriad chapters of California's past, inviting you to explore, learn, and be inspired by the rich and dynamic history of this remarkable state.

How to Use this Guide

Welcome to your comprehensive guide to exploring California! This chapter is dedicated to helping you understand how to effectively use this guide and the interactive map to enhance your travel experience. Let's dive into the simple steps to navigate the book and utilize the digital tools provided, ensuring you have the best adventure possible.

Understanding the Guide's Structure

The guide features 120 of the best destinations across the beautiful state of California, thoughtfully compiled to inspire and facilitate your explorations. These destinations are divided into areas and listed alphabetically. This organization aims to simplify your search process, making it quick and intuitive to locate each destination in the book.

Using the Alphabetical Listings

Since the destination areas are arranged alphabetically, you can easily flip through the guide to find a specific place or browse areas that catch your interest. Each destination entry in the book includes essential information such as:

- A vivid description of the destination.

- The complete address and the nearest major city, giving you a quick geographical context.

- GPS coordinates for precise navigation.

- The best times to visit, helping you plan your trip according to seasonal attractions and weather.

- Details on tolls or access fees, preparing you for any costs associated with your visit.

- Fun trivia to enhance your knowledge and appreciation of each location.

- A link to the official website for up-to-date information.

To further enhance your experience and save time, you can scan these website links using apps like Google Lens to open them directly without the need to type them into a browser. This seamless integration allows for quicker access to the latest information and resources about each destination.

Navigating with the Interactive State Map

Your guide comes equipped with an innovative tool—an interactive map of California that integrates seamlessly with Google Maps. This digital map is pre-loaded with all 120 destinations, offering an effortless way to visualize and plan your journey across the state.

How to Use the Map:

- **Open the Interactive Map:** Start by accessing the digital map through the link provided in your guide. You can open it on any device that supports Google Maps, such as a smartphone, tablet, or computer.

- **Choose Your Starting Point:** Decide where you will begin your adventure. You might start from your current location or another specific point in California.

- **Explore Nearby Destinations:** With the map open, zoom in and out to view the destinations near your starting point. Click on any marker to see a brief description and access quick links for navigation and more details.

- **Plan Your Itinerary:** Based on the destinations close to your chosen start, you can create a personalized itinerary. You can select multiple locations to visit in a day or plan a more extended road trip through various regions.

CALIFORNIA BUCKET LIST

Combining the Book and Map for Best Results

To get the most out of your adventures:

- Cross-Reference: Use the interactive map to spot destinations you are interested in and then refer back to the guidebook for detailed information and insights.

- Plan Sequentially: As you plan your route on the map, use the alphabetical listing in the book to easily gather information on each destination and organize your visits efficiently.

- Stay Updated: Regularly check the provided website links for any changes in operation hours, fees, or special events at the destinations.

By following these guidelines and utilizing both the guidebook and the interactive map, you will be well-equipped to explore California's diverse landscapes and attractions.

Whether you are seeking solitude in nature, adventure in the outdoors, or cultural experiences in urban settings, this guide will serve as your reliable companion, ensuring every adventure is memorable and every discovery is enriching. Happy travels!

ANAHEIM

Angel Stadium of Anaheim

Feel the thrill of Major League Baseball at Angel Stadium of Anaheim, the home field of the Los Angeles Angels. This iconic stadium, known for its distinctive Big A scoreboard, offers fans an exhilarating experience with a panoramic view of the action on the field. Located in Anaheim, California, Angel Stadium has been a legendary baseball venue since 1966.

You can immerse yourself in the game's atmosphere, savor some ballpark snacks, and maybe even catch a home run ball! Don't miss the unique opportunity to enjoy a fireworks show after select games—it's a fan favorite!

Location: 2000 E Gene Autry Way, Anaheim, CA 92806-6143

Closest City or Town: Anaheim, California

How to Get There: From Interstate 5 (I-5), take exit 109A for Gene Autry Way, and follow the signs to the stadium.

GPS Coordinates: 33.7998135° N, 117.8824162° W

Best Time to Visit: During the MLB season, from April to October

Pass/Permit/Fees: Ticket prices vary depending on the game and seating choice; please visit their website for details.

Did You Know? Angel Stadium is the fourth oldest active Major League Baseball stadium, opening in the same year as the beatles performed at nearby Dodger Stadium.

Website: https://www.cityexperiences.com/san-francisco/city-cruises/alcatraz/?utm_source=google&utm_medium=organic&utm_campaign=alcatraz-city-cruises-google-listing

Disney California Adventure Park

Embark on a spectacular journey through the magic of Disney at Disney California Adventure Park. Located adjacent to Disneyland Park in Anaheim, California, this vibrant theme park brings famous

Pixar and Marvel characters to life. Step into various themed lands and experience thrilling rides, dazzling shows, and delicious dining options.

You can race through Radiator Springs, soar over California landscapes on Soarin','' or immerse yourself in the wizarding world of Doctor Strange. Special highlights include the spectacular World of Color water show and seasonal events like the Lunar New Year Celebration.

Location: 1313 Disneyland Drive, Anaheim, CA 92803-3232

Closest City or Town: Anaheim, California

How to Get There: Accessible via Interstate 5; take Katella Avenue exit and follow the signs to Disneyland Resort.

GPS Coordinates: 33.8064258° N, 117.9185267° W

Best Time to Visit: Weekdays during the fall and winter months for shorter wait times, although holidays and events can be quite magical as well.

Pass/Permit/Fees: Ticket prices range based on age and ticket type; check the website for latest pricing.

Did You Know? The park originally opened on February 8, 2001, following a major reimagining of the area known as Disney's California Adventure Park.

Website: http://disneyland.disney.go.com/destinations/disney-california-adventure/?CMP=OKC-dlr_TA_173

Disneyland Park

Discover the enchanting world of Disneyland Park, where dreams come to life and fairy tales are real. Located in Anaheim, California, this iconic theme park created by Walt Disney himself has been captivating visitors since 1955. Wander through its eight themed lands, each offering unique experiences and attractions.

From the thrilling drops of Space Mountain to the nostalgic charm of It's a Small World, there's something for everyone. And don't miss meeting beloved Disney characters, watching the magical parades, or staying for the nightly fireworks that light up the sky over Sleeping Beauty Castle.

Location: 1313 Disneyland Dr, Anaheim, CA 92802

Closest City or Town: Anaheim, California

How to Get There: Conveniently located off Interstate 5; follow Disneyland Drive and look for signs directing you to the park entrance.

GPS Coordinates: 33.8147415° N, 117.9175740° W

Best Time to Visit: Mid-week during the non-peak seasons (January through March, and September through early December)

Pass/Permit/Fees: Tickets vary in price; see the official site for detailed price information.

Did You Know? Disneyland Park was the only theme park designed and built to completion under the direct supervision of Walt Disney.

Website: https://disneyland.disney.go.com/

Downtown Disney District

Unleash your inner child and experience the lively entertainment, dining, and shopping at Downtown Disney District! Located in Anaheim, California, just outside the gates of Disneyland Resort, this vibrant promenade offers a plethora of activities for all ages.

Enjoy a gourmet meal, shop for exclusive Disney merchandise, or watch live music performances. With its eclectic atmosphere and dynamic events, from seasonal festivities to exciting nightlife, Downtown Disney is the perfect destination for a fun-filled day or evening out.

Location: Disneyland Dr at Katella Ave, Anaheim, CA 92804

Closest City or Town: Anaheim, California

How to Get There: Accessible from Interstate 5, exit at Disneyland Drive/Katella Avenue and follow the signs.

GPS Coordinates: 33.8097925° N, 117.9237869° W

Best Time to Visit: Evenings and weekends offer a lively experience, while weekday mornings are perfect for a more relaxed visit.

Pass/Permit/Fees: No entrance fee; individual shop, dining, and entertainment prices vary.

Did You Know? Downtown Disney District features the WonderGround Gallery, a unique space dedicated to Disney-themed art from local artists.

Website: https://disneyland.disney.go.com/experience-updates/downtown-disney/

BUENA PARK

Knott's Berry Farm

Discover a world of excitement and nostalgia at Knott's Berry Farm, a beloved amusement park located in Buena Park, California. Originally a berry farm, Knott's transformed into a family-friendly destination with thrilling rides, live entertainment, and historical exhibits celebrating its rich heritage. Located just a short drive from Los Angeles, visitors can immerse themselves in roller coasters, enjoy a classic fried chicken dinner, or take a stroll through Ghost Town.

Location: 8039 Beach Blvd, Buena Park, CA 90620-3225

Closest City or Town: Buena Park, California

How to Get There: From I-5 South, take the Beach Blvd exit and head south until you reach the park. Signs will guide you to parking areas.

GPS Coordinates: 33.8443038° N, 118.0002265° W

Best Time to Visit: Spring and fall when the weather is mild and crowds are smaller.

Pass/Permit/Fees: Varies by ticket type; check the website for pricing details.

Did You Know? Knott's Berry Farm is home to the iconic Boysenberry, which was first cultivated here.

Website: http://www.knotts.com/

CALISTOGA

Castello di Amorosa

Step into a medieval dream at Castello di Amorosa, a magnificent 13th-century-inspired winery in Calistoga, California. Complete with drawbridges and dungeons, this castle transports visitors to old-world Italy in the heart of Napa Valley. Indulge in exquisite wine tastings while exploring its grand halls, lush vineyards, and panoramic views of the surrounding countryside.

Location: 4045 Saint Helena Hwy, Calistoga, CA 94515-9609

Closest City or Town: Calistoga, California

How to Get There: From Highway 29 North, follow the signs for Castello di Amorosa, located just south of Calistoga.

GPS Coordinates: 38.5589158° N, 122.5412268° W

Best Time to Visit: Harvest season in the fall for a full winery experience.

Pass/Permit/Fees: Wine tasting fees apply; check the website for tour and tasting packages.

Did You Know? The castle was built over 15 years using medieval construction techniques and imported European materials.

Website: http://www.castellodiamorosa.com/)

CAMBRIA

Moonstone Beach

Embrace coastal serenity at Moonstone Beach in Cambria, California. This idyllic beach offers a picturesque setting with shimmering pebbles, tide pools teeming with marine life, and a scenic boardwalk perfect for leisurely strolls. Located along the rugged central coast, it's a peaceful escape for nature enthusiasts and beachcombers alike.

Location: 5885 Moonstone Beach Dr, Cambria, CA 93428

Closest City or Town: Cambria, California

How to Get There: From Highway 1, take the Moonstone Beach Drive exit and follow the signs to the beach parking area.

GPS Coordinates: 35.5695380° N, 121.1102700° W

Best Time to Visit: Summer and early fall for the best weather and tide-pooling opportunities.

Pass/Permit/Fees: Free access to the beach.

Did You Know? Moonstone Beach is known for its polished stones, including agates and jaspers, which give the beach its name.

Website: https://en.wikipedia.org/wiki/Moonstone_Beach

CARLSBAD

LEGOLAND California

Enter a world of imagination at LEGOLAND California, a colorful theme park in Carlsbad, California. Tailored for families and LEGO enthusiasts, this park features interactive rides, stunning LEGO sculptures, and themed lands that bring LEGO bricks to life. Located near the Pacific coast, it's an attraction that guarantees fun and creativity for all ages.

Location: 1 Legoland Drive, Carlsbad, CA 92008-4610

Closest City or Town: Carlsbad, California

How to Get There: From I-5, take the Palomar Airport Road exit and follow the signs to the park entrance.

GPS Coordinates: 33.1262496° N, 117.3119239° W

Best Time to Visit: Spring and fall for pleasant weather and fewer crowds.

Pass/Permit/Fees: Admission fees vary; refer to the website for detailed information.

Did You Know? LEGOLAND California opened in 1999 and features over 60 rides and attractions.

Website: http://california.legoland.com/

CARMEL

Carmel River State Beach

Find your coastal escape at Carmel River State Beach in charming Carmel, California. This tranquil beach offers a serene setting with soft sands, clear waters, and abundant birdlife. A popular spot for kayaking and bird watching, it's a nature lover's paradise with breathtaking ocean views and peaceful surroundings.

Location: 26478 Carmelo St, Carmel, CA 93923

Closest City or Town: Carmel, California

How to Get There: From Highway 1, take the Ocean Avenue exit and follow signs to the beach along Scenic Road.

GPS Coordinates: 36.5373847° N, 121.9279355° W

Best Time to Visit: Year-round, but fall offers the most pleasant weather and fewer tourists.

Pass/Permit/Fees: Free access to the beach.

Did You Know? The beach is part of the Carmel River Lagoon and Wetlands Natural Preserve, protecting a vibrant ecosystem.

Website: http://www.parks.ca.gov/default.asp?page_id=567

Point Lobos

Find your sense of adventure and peace at Point Lobos, often called the crown jewel of California's state parks. Located just south of Carmel along Highway 1, this coastal haven boasts dramatic ocean vistas, hidden coves, and a unique mix of land and marine wildlife. Hike the miles of trails that meander through the forest and along the craggy shorelines, or dive into the pristine underwater forests for a scuba adventure. Each turn reveals new wonders, from playful sea otters to scenic overlooks of the Pacific Ocean.

Location: Hwy 1, Carmel, CA 93923

Closest City or Town: Carmel, California

CALIFORNIA BUCKET LIST

How to Get There: Take Highway 1 South from Carmel and look for the entrance signs to Point Lobos State Natural Reserve.

GPS Coordinates: 36.5159815° N, 121.9367979° W

Best Time to Visit: Spring and fall offer mild weather and fewer crowds.

Pass/Permit/Fees: $10 vehicle day-use fee; additional fees for diving permits.

Did You Know? The area was once a bustling whaling and abalone cannery during the late 1800s and early 1900s.

Website: https://www.parks.ca.gov/?page_id=571

CORONADO

Coronado Island

Experience coastal charm at its finest on Coronado Island, a gem located just across the bay from bustling San Diego. Known for its iconic Hotel del Coronado, wide sandy beaches, and charming downtown area, it's a haven for relaxation and family-friendly activities. Stroll along Orange Avenue for boutique shopping, dine at waterside eateries, or rent a bike and explore the scenic Silver Strand. Don't miss the opportunity to kayak or paddleboard in the calm waters of Glorietta Bay for a unique perspective of this enchanting locale.

Location: 1063 Ocean Blvd, Coronado, CA 92118

Closest City or Town: San Diego, California

How to Get There: Cross the iconic Coronado Bridge from San Diego or take the ferry from downtown to Coronado Ferry Landing.

GPS Coordinates: 32.6826701° N, 117.1809013° W

Best Time to Visit: Year-round, but summer offers the best beach weather.

Pass/Permit/Fees: Free to visit, but some activities may require rentals or fees.

Did You Know? The Hotel del Coronado has hosted numerous U.S. presidents and celebrities since its opening in 1888.

Website: https://coronadovisitorcenter.com/

DEATH VALLEY NATIONAL PARK

Badwater

Step into a surreal landscape at Badwater Basin, the lowest point in North America, located within Death Valley National Park. At 282 feet below sea level, this otherworldly salt flat stretches as far as the eye can see, creating a desolate beauty unlike any other. Visitors can walk out onto the vast, hexagon-shaped salt crust, feeling as though they are on another planet. Heat and aridity dominate here, so plan your visit carefully and experience the stark, raw beauty of this iconic desert location.

Location: Badwater Rd. 19 mi south of Furnace Creek, Death Valley National Park, CA 92328

Closest City or Town: Furnace Creek, California

How to Get There: From Furnace Creek, drive 19 miles south on Badwater Road until you reach the parking area for Badwater Basin.

GPS Coordinates: 36.1069403° N, 116.7347976° W

Best Time to Visit: Fall through early spring to avoid extreme summer heat.

Pass/Permit/Fees: National Park entrance fees apply.

Did You Know? The salt flats cover nearly 200 square miles, making it the largest protected salt flat in the world.

Website: http://www.nps.gov/deva/index.htm

Dante's View

For a breathtaking panorama of Death Valley, head to Dante's View, perched over 5,000 feet above the valley floor. This overlook offers an unparalleled vantage point to observe the vastness of one of the hottest places on earth. On a clear day, you can view both the highest point in the contiguous United States, Mount Whitney, and the lowest point, Badwater Basin. Ideal for sunrise or sunset, the vistas from Dante's View are nothing short of awe-inspiring, providing a dramatic contrast to the stark desert landscape below.

Location: Dante's View Road, Death Valley National Park, CA 92328

Closest City or Town: Furnace Creek, California

How to Get There: From Furnace Creek, take Highway 190 East and turn right onto Dante's View Road; follow this road to the top.

GPS Coordinates: 36.2205786° N, 116.7265978° W

Best Time to Visit: Spring and fall when temperatures are moderate.

Pass/Permit/Fees: National Park entrance fees apply.

Did You Know? The overlook was used in the original Star Wars movie to depict the planet Tatooine.

Website:https://www.nps.gov/deva/learn/photosmultimedia/dantes-view.htm

Zabriskie Point

Soak in the surreal beauty of Zabriskie Point, one of Death Valley National Park's most photographed spots. This viewpoint provides stunning vistas of the badlands, with its golden-colored, eroded hills creating a dramatic, textured landscape. It's especially mesmerizing at sunrise and sunset when the light casts magical hues over the terrain. Visitors can take a short walk up the paved path to the lookout, where you can see the Panamint Mountains in the distance and the labyrinthine shapes of the badlands below.

Location: Route 190, Death Valley National Park, CA 92328

Closest City or Town: Furnace Creek, California

How to Get There: Follow Route 190 from Furnace Creek east for about 4 miles until signs direct you to the Zabriskie Point parking area.

GPS Coordinates: 36.4200667° N, 116.8122303° W

Best Time to Visit: Sunrise and sunset for the best light and coolest temperatures.

Pass/Permit/Fees: National Park entrance fees apply.

Did You Know? Zabriskie Point is named after Christian Zabriskie, a prominent figure in the Pacific Coast Borax Company that mined the area.

Website: https://www.nps.gov/places/zabriskie-point-scenic-viewpoint.htm

DEL MONTE FOREST

17-Mile Drive

Find your sense of adventure and scenic beauty on the iconic 17-Mile Drive, a breathtaking journey through Del Monte Forest and along the stunning California coastline. Discover enchanting landscapes, majestic coastal cliffs, and the famous Lone Cypress as you meander through this picturesque route. Located in Pebble Beach, this drive offers a unique opportunity to explore some of California's most pristine natural wonders and historic landmarks.

Location: J24R+79 Pebble Beach, Del Monte Forest, California

Closest City or Town: Monterey, California

How to Get There: From Monterey, take CA-1 S and exit on Highway 68 W. Follow the signs to the 17-Mile Drive entrance.

GPS Coordinates: 36.5727577° N, 121.9487170° W

Best Time to Visit: Spring and fall offer mild weather and fewer crowds.

Pass/Permit/Fees: $11.25 entrance fee per vehicle. Motorcycles are not permitted.

Did You Know? The Lone Cypress, one of the most photographed trees in North America, has stood on its rocky perch for over 250 years.

Website: http://www.pebblebeach.com/activities/explore-the-monterey-peninsula/17-mile-drive

ESCONDIDO

San Diego Zoo Safari Park

Embark on a wild adventure at the San Diego Zoo Safari Park, where you can experience the thrill of a safari without leaving California. This expansive wildlife sanctuary in Escondido allows visitors to observe animals roaming freely in large, naturalistic habitats. Located in the scenic San Pasqual Valley, this park is home to a diverse array of species and offers unique experiences like the Africa Tram and Cheetah Run.

Location: 15500 San Pasqual Valley Rd, Escondido, CA 92027-7017

Closest City or Town: Escondido, California

How to Get There: From I-15, take the Via Rancho Parkway exit and follow the signs to the Safari Park.

GPS Coordinates: 33.0997931° N, 116.9922942° W

Best Time to Visit: Spring and fall for pleasant weather and active animals.

Pass/Permit/Fees: General admission varies, starting around $60 for adults.

Did You Know? The Safari Park is home to the largest veterinary hospital in the world.

Website: http://www.sdzsafaripark.org/

LONG BEACH

Aquarium of the Pacific

Dive into the wonders of the ocean at the Aquarium of the Pacific, located in the vibrant coastal city of Long Beach. This world-class aquarium offers a deep dive into the marine ecosystems of the Pacific Ocean, featuring over 12,000 animals and 100 exhibits. Engage with interactive displays, touch pools, and captivating shows that bring the underwater world to life.

Location: 100 Aquarium Way, Long Beach, CA 90802-8126

Closest City or Town: Long Beach, California

How to Get There: Accessible via I-710 S, exit at Shoreline Drive and follow signs to Aquarium Way.

GPS Coordinates: 33.7619735° N, 118.1969738° W

Best Time to Visit: Year-round, though weekdays are less crowded.

Pass/Permit/Fees: General admission starts at $36.95 for adults.

Did You Know? The Aquarium's Pacific Visions wing features a state-of-the-art interactive theater and multimedia exhibits.

Website: http://www.aquariumofpacific.org/

The Queen Mary

Step aboard The Queen Mary, a majestic ocean liner permanently docked in Long Beach, and journey back in time to the golden age of transatlantic travel. This historic ship offers a blend of luxury and intrigue with its art deco design, elegant staterooms, and ghostly legends. Located at the Long Beach harbor, it now serves as a hotel, museum, and attraction, offering guided tours and paranormal investigations.

Location: 1126 Queens Hwy, Long Beach, CA 90802-6331

Closest City or Town: Long Beach, California

CALIFORNIA BUCKET LIST

How to Get There: From I-710 S, take the exit toward Queen Mary and follow the signs.

GPS Coordinates: 33.7517297° N, 118.1905454° W

Best Time to Visit: Fall and winter for a less crowded experience.

Pass/Permit/Fees: Admission varies by tour and activity.

Did You Know? The Queen Mary is said to be one of the most haunted places in America.

Website: https://queenmary.com/tours/tours-exhibits/

Los Angeles

Battleship USS Iowa Museum

Discover the might and history of naval warfare at the Battleship USS Iowa Museum, anchored in San Pedro. This historic battleship, known as the "Battleship of Presidents," served in World War II, the Korean War, and the Cold War. Visitors can explore its decks, see the captain's cabin, and learn about life at sea through interactive exhibits.

Location: 250 S Harbor Blvd San Pedro, Los Angeles, CA 90731-2830

Closest City or Town: San Pedro, California

How to Get There: From I-110 S, exit at Harbor Blvd and follow the signs to the Battleship Iowa.

GPS Coordinates: 33.7422615° N, 118.2772823° W

Best Time to Visit: Year-round, though weekdays are less crowded.

Pass/Permit/Fees: General admission starts at $22.95 for adults.

Did You Know? The USS Iowa was the only battleship with a bathtub installed for a president.

Website: http://www.pacificbattleship.com/

California Science Center

Unlock the mysteries of science and innovation at the California Science Center in Los Angeles. This dynamic hub invites visitors of all ages to explore interactive exhibits, witness space shuttles up close, and engage in hands-on experiments. Located in Exposition Park, the center offers a comprehensive journey through various scientific fields, from space exploration to ecosystems. You can watch an IMAX film, explore the wonders of the universe, and even step inside real-life space capsules. Don't miss the inspiring presentation of the Space Shuttle Endeavour!

Location: 700 Exposition Park Drive, Los Angeles, CA 90037-1254

Closest City or Town: Los Angeles, California

How to Get There: From downtown Los Angeles, take the I-110 South and exit at Exposition Blvd., then follow signs to Exposition Park.

GPS Coordinates: 34.0159905° N, 118.2861447° W

Best Time to Visit: Year-round, with weekdays offering fewer crowds.

Pass/Permit/Fees: General admission is free; special exhibits and IMAX may have fees.

Did You Know? The California Science Center is the permanent home of the space shuttle Endeavour.

Website: https://www.facebook.com/CaliforniaScienceCenter/

Crypto.com Arena

Feel the adrenaline rush at Crypto.com Arena, an iconic venue for sports and entertainment in downtown Los Angeles. Home to the Lakers, Clippers, Kings, and Sparks, it's a hotspot for electrifying basketball, hockey games, and awe-inspiring concerts. Located on Figueroa Street, this modern arena hosts over 250 events annually, making it a must-visit for sports enthusiasts and music lovers alike. Enjoy world-class entertainment, gourmet concessions, and an unforgettable atmosphere inside this state-of-the-art facility.

Location: 1111 S Figueroa St, Los Angeles, CA 90015-1300

Closest City or Town: Los Angeles, California

How to Get There: From I-10, take the Grand Ave exit, then follow signs to Crypto.com Arena located on Figueroa Street.

GPS Coordinates: 34.0430058° N, 118.2673597° W

Best Time to Visit: During major sporting events, concerts, and shows.

Pass/Permit/Fees: Event ticket prices vary; check the website for details.

Did You Know? Crypto.com Arena was formerly known as Staples Center until 2021.

Website: https://www.cryptoarena.com/

Dodger Stadium

Catch the thrill of Major League Baseball at Dodger Stadium, an iconic venue nestled in the heart of Los Angeles. As the oldest ballpark in the MLB, it offers a nostalgic yet exhilarating experience for fans of the Los Angeles Dodgers. Located on Vin Scully Avenue, the stadium provides panoramic views of downtown LA and the San Gabriel Mountains. You can enjoy ballpark snacks, cheer on your team, and soak in the vibrant atmosphere. Make sure to join in on the singing of Take Me Out to the Ballgame during the seventh-inning stretch!

Location: 1000 Vin Scully Avenue, Los Angeles, CA 90012

Closest City or Town: Los Angeles, California

How to Get There: From downtown Los Angeles, take the CA-110 North and exit onto Stadium Way, following the signs to Dodger Stadium.

GPS Coordinates: 34.0735795° N, 118.2404671° W

Best Time to Visit: During the MLB season, from April to October.

Pass/Permit/Fees: Ticket prices vary by game and seating; check the website.

Did You Know? Dodger Stadium is the largest MLB stadium by seating capacity, accommodating 56,000 fans.

Website: https://www.mlb.com/dodgers/ballpark/transportation

Griffith Observatory

Explore the cosmos at Griffith Observatory, a gateway to the stars in Los Angeles. This iconic landmark provides unparalleled views of the city and the universe beyond. Located atop Mount Hollywood in Griffith Park, the observatory offers fascinating exhibits, telescopes for public use, and captivating planetarium shows. Visitors can engage in stargazing, attend educational events, and enjoy the stunning vista that stretches from downtown LA to the Pacific Ocean. The observatory also features the renowned Zeiss Telescope, which has been in use since 1935.

Location: 2800 E. Observatory Rd., Los Angeles, CA 90027-1299

Closest City or Town: Los Angeles, California

How to Get There: Take the I-5 North to Los Feliz Blvd, then follow the signs to Griffith Park and the observatory.

GPS Coordinates: 34.1184070° N, 118.3004219° W

Best Time to Visit: Evenings for optimal stargazing; weekdays to avoid crowds.

Pass/Permit/Fees: Free general admission; planetarium shows have a fee.

Did You Know? Griffith Observatory has appeared in countless films, including the iconic Rebel Without a Cause starring James Dean.

Website: http://www.griffithobservatory.org/

Griffith Park

Find your escape in nature at Griffith Park, one of the largest urban parks in North America. Nestled in Los Angeles, this green haven boasts over 4,000 acres of rugged terrain, scenic trails, and diverse attractions. Visitors can hike to the Griffith Observatory, explore the Los Angeles Zoo, and ride the historic Merry-Go-Round. With its vast open spaces and panoramic city views, the park caters to nature lovers, fitness enthusiasts, and families. Don't miss the chance to hike to the iconic Hollywood Sign for a quintessential LA experience.

Location: 4730 Crystal Springs Drive, Los Angeles, CA 90027-1401

Closest City or Town: Los Angeles, California

How to Get There: From downtown LA, take the I-5 North, exit at Los Feliz Blvd, and follow the signs to Griffith Park.

GPS Coordinates: 34.1365544° N, 118.2942000° W

Best Time to Visit: Year-round; early mornings for cooler temperatures and quietude.

Pass/Permit/Fees: Free entrance; specific attractions may have fees.

Did You Know? Griffith Park is home to the famous Greek Theatre, an open-air amphitheater hosting concerts and events.

Website: https://www.laparks.org/griffithpark/

Hollywood Sign

Gaze upon the iconic Hollywood Sign, a symbol of the entertainment industry and a must-visit for anyone exploring Los Angeles. Nestled on the southern slope of Mount Lee, this landmark offers an incredible vista of the sprawling city below. Hike the scenic trails of Griffith Park to get up close to the sign and capture the quintessential Hollywood photo.

Location: 4MMH+J9 Los Angeles, California

Closest City or Town: Los Angeles, California

How to Get There: From downtown Los Angeles, take the US-101 N and exit at Gower St. Follow the signs to Griffith Park and make your way to the recommended viewpoints.

GPS Coordinates: 34.1341151° N, 118.3215482° W

Best Time to Visit: Early mornings or late afternoons for the best light and cooler temperatures.

Pass/Permit/Fees: Free access.

Did You Know? The Hollywood Sign originally read Hollywoodland as part of an advertisement for a real estate development.

Website: http://www.visitcalifornia.com/attraction/hollywood-sign

Hollywood Walk of Fame

Stroll down the Hollywood Walk of Fame and immerse yourself in the glitz and glamour of Hollywood's entertainment history. Located along Hollywood Boulevard and Vine Street, this star-studded sidewalk features over 2,600 brass stars commemorating legends of film, television, music, and theater. Every step you take brings you closer to the magic of the big screen and the stars themselves.

Location: Hollywood Blvd at Vine St, Los Angeles, CA 90028

Closest City or Town: Los Angeles, California

How to Get There: From US-101, take the Hollywood Blvd exit and head west. The Walk of Fame stretches along Hollywood Blvd and Vine St.

GPS Coordinates: 34.0985259° N, 118.3255647° W

Best Time to Visit: Visit on weekday mornings to avoid the crowds.

Pass/Permit/Fees: Free access.

Did You Know? The Hollywood Walk of Fame was established in 1960, and Joanne Woodward received the first star.

Website: http://www.walkoffame.com/

La Brea Tar Pits and Museum

Discover the prehistoric past at the La Brea Tar Pits and Museum, where Ice Age fossils have been unearthed in the heart of Los Angeles. Located on Wilshire Boulevard, this site offers a fascinating glimpse into ancient history with live excavation sites, interactive exhibits, and a chance to see the tar pits bubbling up from the ground.

Location: 5801 Wilshire Blvd, Los Angeles, CA 90036-4539

Closest City or Town: Los Angeles, California

How to Get There: Take Wilshire Blvd west from US-101 and follow signs to the La Brea Tar Pits and Museum.

GPS Coordinates: 34.0638800° N, 118.3564450° W

Best Time to Visit: Spring and fall for pleasant weather and fewer crowds.

Pass/Permit/Fees: Admission fees apply; check the website for details.

Did You Know? More than 3.5 million fossils have been discovered at this site, including specimens from mammoths, saber-toothed cats, and dire wolves.

Website: http://www.tarpits.org/

Los Angeles County Museum of Art (LACMA)

Immerse yourself in the world of art at the Los Angeles County Museum of Art (LACMA), the largest art museum in the western United States. Located on Wilshire Boulevard, this cultural hub boasts a diverse collection spanning ancient to contemporary art. Wander through the iconic Urban Light installation and explore masterpieces from around the globe.

Location: 5905 Wilshire Blvd, Los Angeles, CA 90036-4597

Closest City or Town: Los Angeles, California

How to Get There: From US-101, take the Highland Ave exit and head south to Wilshire Blvd. Follow the signs to LACMA.

GPS Coordinates: 34.0637913° N, 118.3588851° W

Best Time to Visit: Visit on weekdays to enjoy a quieter experience.

Pass/Permit/Fees: Admission fees apply; check the website for details.

Did You Know? LACMA's Urban Light is composed of 202 vintage street lamps, collected by artist Chris Burden.

Website: http://www.lacma.org/

Madame Tussauds Hollywood

Step into the world of celebrity at Madame Tussauds Hollywood, where life-like wax figures of your favorite stars await. Located on Hollywood Boulevard, this attraction offers a unique blend of history, glamour, and fun. Pose with A-listers, historical figures, and pop culture icons, making for an unforgettable visit.

Location: 6933 Hollywood Blvd, Los Angeles, CA 90028-6146

Closest City or Town: Los Angeles, California

How to Get There: From US-101, take the Highland Ave exit and head south to Hollywood Blvd.

GPS Coordinates: 34.1017225° N, 118.3415065° W

Best Time to Visit: Weekdays for shorter lines and a less crowded experience.

Pass/Permit/Fees: Admission fees apply; check the website for details.

Did You Know? Madame Tussauds Hollywood has over 100 wax figures, each taking up to six months to create.

Website: http://www.madametussauds.com/hollywood

Petersen Automotive Museum

Unleash your inner car enthusiast at the Petersen Automotive Museum, a haven for automotive history and design. Located in the vibrant city of Los Angeles, this museum showcases an extensive collection of rare and iconic vehicles from different eras. Visitors can marvel at vintage cars, futuristic designs, and even movie star vehicles. The museum also offers interactive exhibits and a rotating display of unique cars, making it an ever-evolving destination for any automobile lover.

Location: 6060 Wilshire Blvd, Los Angeles, CA 90036-3605

Closest City or Town: Los Angeles, California

How to Get There: From downtown Los Angeles, take I-10 W to S Fairfax Ave, then turn right onto Wilshire Blvd.

GPS Coordinates: 34.0620240° N, 118.3613631° W

Best Time to Visit: Open year-round, with weekdays offering fewer crowds.

Pass/Permit/Fees: General admission fees apply; check the website for current ticket prices.

Did You Know? The Petersen Automotive Museum has a unique facade designed to look like stainless steel ribbons swirling around it.

Website: http://www.petersen.org/

Rodeo Drive

Wander through the heart of luxury and style on Rodeo Drive, an iconic shopping street located in Beverly Hills. This famed boulevard is synonymous with high-end fashion, where you can browse exclusive boutiques and designer flagships. Beyond shopping, Rodeo Drive offers a glimpse into the glamorous lifestyle of Hollywood stars. Take a stroll along its palm-lined sidewalks, enjoy fine dining, and experience the essence of luxury.

Location: Santa Monica Blvd at Wilshire Blvd, Beverly Hills, CA 90210

Closest City or Town: Beverly Hills, California

How to Get There: From downtown Los Angeles, take I-10 W, then exit onto S La Cienega Blvd to Wilshire Blvd.

GPS Coordinates: 34.0709683° N, 118.4047126° W

Best Time to Visit: Year-round, but weekdays are best for a leisurely visit.

Pass/Permit/Fees: Free to visit, although shopping and dining prices vary.

Did You Know? Rodeo Drive was featured prominently in the movie Pretty Woman, starring Julia Roberts.

Website: https://www.rodeodrive-bh.com/

TCL Chinese Theatres

Step into the star-studded legacy of Hollywood at TCL Chinese Theatres, a legendary movie palace on Hollywood Boulevard. Opened in 1927, this iconic landmark is renowned for its grand architecture and the forecourt of handprints and footprints left by film legends. Visitors can enjoy blockbuster films in its state-of-the-art auditorium, take guided tours, and soak in the history of Tinseltown.

Location: 6925 Hollywood Boulevard, Los Angeles, CA 90028-6103

Closest City or Town: Los Angeles, California

How to Get There: From downtown Los Angeles, take US-101 N, exit at Hollywood Blvd, and drive west.

GPS Coordinates: 34.1020231° N, 118.3409712° W

Best Time to Visit: Year-round, with evening showings offering a festive atmosphere.

Pass/Permit/Fees: Admission fees vary based on the movie; guided tours have separate fees.

Did You Know? TCL Chinese Theatres hosts the annual Oscar night red carpet and premiere events.

Website: http://www.tclchinesetheatres.com/

The Broad

Discover the cutting edge of contemporary art at The Broad, a modern art museum in downtown Los Angeles. This innovative space features a stunning collection of post-war and contemporary works from around the globe. Visitors can explore free exhibits, participate in interactive installations, and enjoy the striking architecture of the building itself, designed by Diller Scofidio + Renfro.

Location: 221 S Grand Ave, Los Angeles, CA 90012-3020

Closest City or Town: Los Angeles, California

How to Get There: From downtown Los Angeles, head northwest on W 1st St, then turn right onto S Grand Ave.

GPS Coordinates: 34.0545021° N, 118.2501802° W

Best Time to Visit: Weekdays, especially mornings, to avoid large crowds.

Pass/Permit/Fees: Free general admission; special exhibits may have fees.

Did You Know? The Broad's honeycomb-like exterior is known as the veil, covering the building's structure.

Website: http://www.thebroad.org/

The Getty Center

Marvel at art and admire panoramic views at The Getty Center, an iconic cultural institution in the hills overlooking Los Angeles. Home to an extensive collection of European paintings, sculptures, and decorative arts, the Getty also features modern architecture and beautifully landscaped gardens. Art lovers can stroll through awe-inspiring galleries, relax in the Central Garden, and enjoy educational programs.

Location: 1200 Getty Center Dr, Los Angeles, CA 90049

Closest City or Town: Los Angeles, California

How to Get There: From downtown Los Angeles, take I-405 N and exit at Getty Center Dr.

GPS Coordinates: 34.0773438° N, 118.4732648° W

Best Time to Visit: Weekdays for a quieter experience; late afternoon for golden hour views.

Pass/Permit/Fees: Free admission, but parking fees apply.

Did You Know? The Central Garden at the Getty Center was designed by artist Robert Irwin and is considered a living sculpture.

Website: http://www.getty.edu/visit/center

The Wizarding World of Harry Potter

Step into the enchanting world of sorcery at The Wizarding World of Harry Potter, located within Universal Studios Hollywood in Universal City, California. Here, fans of J.K. Rowling's magical universe can explore the iconic Hogwarts Castle, walk through Hogsmeade village, and experience thrilling rides like Harry Potter and the Forbidden Journey. Indulge in a frothy butterbeer, shop for wands at Ollivanders, and immerse yourself in spellbinding shows. Magic comes to life around every corner, creating an unforgettable experience for wizards young and old.

Location: 100 Universal City Plaza, Universal City, CA 91608

Closest City or Town: Universal City, California

How to Get There: From US-101, take the Universal Studios Blvd exit, follow the signs to Universal Studios Hollywood.

GPS Coordinates: 34.138195° N, 118.353883° W

Best Time to Visit: Weekdays in early spring or late fall for lighter crowds.

Pass/Permit/Fees: Park admission fees apply; check the website for detailed ticket information.

Did You Know?: The park features a life-size replica of the Hogwarts Express, complete with steam and whistle sounds.

Website: http://www.universalstudioshollywood.com/harrypotter/

Union Station

Journey into the architectural splendor of Union Station, a historic gateway to Los Angeles' bustling downtown. As one of the last great

American rail stations, it seamlessly blends Art Deco, Mission Revival, and Dutch Colonial styles. Wander through the grand halls, admire the stunning tilework, or relax in the tranquil garden patio. Union Station is not just a transit hub; it's a vibrant cultural landmark offering a glimpse into the golden age of rail travel.

Location: 800 N Alameda St, Los Angeles, CA 90012-2177

Closest City or Town: Los Angeles, California

How to Get There: Accessible via I-10, exit at Alameda Street, and follow signs to Union Station.

GPS Coordinates: 34.0560324° N, 118.2366600° W

Best Time to Visit: Anytime, though early mornings provide a quieter experience.

Pass/Permit/Fees: Free access to the station; transportation fees apply.

Did You Know?: Union Station has been featured in numerous films, including Blade Runner and Catch Me If You Can.

Website: http://unionstationla.com/

Universal CityWalk Hollywood

Immerse yourself in the vibrant atmosphere of Universal CityWalk Hollywood, a bustling promenade located adjacent to Universal Studios Hollywood in Los Angeles. This dynamic entertainment district offers an array of dining, shopping, and live music experiences. Enjoy a meal at world-class restaurants, shop for unique souvenirs, or catch a concert at the outdoor stage. The neon-lit walkways and eclectic ambiance make Universal CityWalk a must-visit destination for day and night.

Location: 100 Universal City Plaza, Los Angeles, CA 91608

Closest City or Town: Los Angeles, California

How to Get There: From US-101, take the Universal Studios Blvd exit and follow signs to CityWalk.

GPS Coordinates: 34.1361697° N, 118.3537322° W

Best Time to Visit: Evenings for a lively experience; weekdays for fewer crowds.

Pass/Permit/Fees: Free admission; parking fees and individual retail prices apply.

Did You Know?: Universal CityWalk features one of the largest IMAX theaters in the world.

Website: https://www.universalstudioshollywood.com/web/en/us/things-to-do/lands/citywalk

Universal Studios Hollywood

Unlock a world of cinematic wonders at Universal Studios Hollywood, where blockbuster films and thrilling rides converge. Whether you're braving the raptor encounters in Jurassic World, exploring the magical sights of the Wizarding World of Harry Potter, or journeying through the exciting studio tour, every corner promises adventure and nostalgia. This dynamic theme park offers a blend of groundbreaking attractions and behind-the-scenes entertainment experiences, making it an iconic destination for film enthusiasts.

Location: 100 Universal City Plaza, Los Angeles, CA 91608-1002

Closest City or Town: Los Angeles, California

How to Get There: From US-101, take the Universal Studios Blvd exit, and follow signs to the park entrance.

GPS Coordinates: 34.1388816° N, 118.3555544° W

Best Time to Visit: Weekdays in autumn or spring to avoid peak crowds.

Pass/Permit/Fees: Park admission required; visit the website for ticket prices.

Did You Know?: Universal Studios Hollywood is home to the world-famous Studio Tour, which takes you behind the scenes of a working film studio.

Website: http://www.universalstudioshollywood.com/

Venice Beach Boardwalk

Soak up the eclectic vibes at Venice Beach Boardwalk, a cultural hotspot located along the Pacific coastline of Los Angeles. This iconic destination offers a lively atmosphere with street performers, eclectic shops, and free-spirited visitors. Explore the vibrant murals, enjoy a game of basketball at the courts, or watch skateboarders at the famous skatepark. With its bohemian charm and lively beachfront activities, Venice Beach Boardwalk captures the quintessential Southern California lifestyle.

Location: 1800 Ocean Front Walk, Los Angeles, CA 90291

Closest City or Town: Los Angeles, California

How to Get There: From I-10, take the exit for Lincoln Blvd, head west on Venice Blvd, and follow signs to the beach.

GPS Coordinates: 33.9856758° N, 118.4727856° W

Best Time to Visit: Late spring through early fall for sunny weather and beach activities.

Pass/Permit/Fees: Free access; parking fees may apply.

Did You Know?: Venice Beach is often referred to as Muscle Beach for its iconic outdoor gym where bodybuilders, including Arnold Schwarzenegger, have trained.

Website: http://www.laparks.org/venice

Venice Canals Walkway

Stroll through a slice of Europe without leaving California at the Venice Canals Walkway. Located in the vibrant neighborhood of Venice Beach, Los Angeles, these picturesque canals were inspired by Venice, Italy, and offer a tranquil escape amidst the urban hustle. You can leisurely walk along the charming canal paths, marvel at the quaint bridges, and admire the beautifully landscaped gardens and eclectic homes. This idyllic setting invites you to take a serene gondola ride or simply enjoy the peace and beauty of this unique L.A. hidden gem.

Location: Washington Blvd Dell Ave & Court A, Los Angeles, CA 90292

Closest City or Town: Los Angeles, California

How to Get There: From I-10 West, take the Lincoln Blvd exit south toward Venice and turn right on Washington Blvd. Follow signs to the Venice Canals Walkway.

GPS Coordinates: 33.9833582° N, 118.4675949° W

Best Time to Visit: Spring and fall for pleasant weather

Pass/Permit/Fees: Free access

Did You Know? The canals were built in 1905 by Abbot Kinney to recreate the appearance of Venice, Italy.

Website: http://www.hmdb.org/m.asp?m=178246

Walt Disney Concert Hall

Get lost in the captivating world of music and architecture at the Walt Disney Concert Hall. Situated in downtown Los Angeles, this Frank Gehry-designed masterpiece offers unparalleled acoustics and a stunning visual experience. You can attend a performance by the Los Angeles Philharmonic, explore the striking stainless steel exterior, and marvel at the grandeur of the concert hall. Beyond concerts, you can enjoy guided tours that reveal behind-the-scenes insights into this cultural icon.

Location: 111 S Grand Ave, Los Angeles, CA 90012-3034

Closest City or Town: Los Angeles, California

How to Get There: Located in downtown LA, accessible from I-110 South by taking the 4th St/3rd St exit to Grand Ave.

GPS Coordinates: 34.0553468° N, 118.2499213° W

Best Time to Visit: Year-round, with prime concert seasons in fall and spring

Pass/Permit/Fees: Tour and concert ticket prices vary; please check the website.

Did You Know? The concert hall's stainless steel curves have contributed to it becoming one of Gehry's most famous works.

Website: http://www.laphil.com/

MALIBU

The Getty Villa

Step back into ancient times at The Getty Villa in Malibu, a breathtaking museum and educational center dedicated to the arts and cultures of ancient Greece, Rome, and Etruria. This reconstructed Roman country house offers you the chance to explore extensive gardens, architectural marvels, and timeless art collections. Nestled in the Pacific Palisades, the Villa's coastal views and serene ambiance make it a perfect cultural escape.

Location: 17985 Pacific Coast Highway Pacific Palisades, Malibu, CA 90272

Closest City or Town: Malibu, California

How to Get There: From the Pacific Coast Highway, the Villa is accessible south of Malibu; simply follow signs to the grounds.

GPS Coordinates: 34.0458857° N, 118.5648608° W

Best Time to Visit: Spring and fall for optimal weather

Pass/Permit/Fees: Entry is free, but timed tickets are required; parking fees apply.

Did You Know? The Villa's design is inspired by the Villa dei Papiri, an ancient Roman luxury villa.

Website: http://www.getty.edu/visit

MILL VALLEY

Muir Woods National Monument

Discover the tranquility of towering redwoods at Muir Woods National Monument, just north of San Francisco in Mill Valley. This enchanting forest offers visitors a chance to walk beneath some of the tallest trees in the world, taking in the forest's serenity and natural beauty. Meandering trails and educational exhibits add to the experience, making it a perfect getaway for nature lovers and those looking to escape the hustle and bustle of city life.

Location: 1 Muir Woods Rd, Mill Valley, CA 94941-4205

Closest City or Town: Mill Valley, California

How to Get There: Take US-101 North from San Francisco, exit onto CA-1 North, and follow signs for Muir Woods.

GPS Coordinates: 37.8934812° N, 122.5728376° W

Best Time to Visit: Spring and fall for the best weather

Pass/Permit/Fees: $15 entrance fee; free for children under 15

Did You Know? Muir Woods was declared a national monument in 1908 by President Theodore Roosevelt.

Website: http://www.nps.gov/muwo/index.htm

MONTEREY

Cannery Row

Immerse yourself in history and charm along Cannery Row, located on the scenic waterfront of Monterey. Once the heart of the sardine-packing industry, today it has been transformed into a vibrant seaside area filled with restaurants, shops, and attractions. Explore the historic sites, visit the world-class Monterey Bay Aquarium, and enjoy waterfront dining as you soak in the stunning coastal views. Cannery Row's rich history and lively atmosphere make it a must-visit destination.

Location: Cannery Row & Wave Streets 700 Cannery Row, Monterey, CA 93940

Closest City or Town: Monterey, California

How to Get There: From US-101, take the Monterey Peninsula Exit, follow Del Monte Ave to Lighthouse Ave, and turn onto Cannery Row.

GPS Coordinates: 36.6162117° N, 121.9004171° W

Best Time to Visit: Spring through fall for pleasant weather

Pass/Permit/Fees: Free access, some attractions and parking may have fees

Did You Know? Cannery Row was the setting for several novels by John Steinbeck, including the famous Cannery Row.

Website: http://www.canneryrow.com/

Monterey Bay

Discover the scenic wonder of Monterey Bay, nestled along California's picturesque central coast. Known for its stunning marine habitats and diverse wildlife, this bay is a haven for nature enthusiasts. You can take a whale-watching cruise, explore the tide pools, or just relax on the sandy beaches. The bay's crystal-clear waters are perfect for kayaking and scuba diving, offering glimpses of sea lions, otters, and various seabirds. Monterey Bay connects you directly to the Pacific Ocean's natural beauty, making it an essential stop for outdoor adventurers and wildlife lovers.

Location: J453+PV Monterey, California

Closest City or Town: Monterey, California

How to Get There: From US-101, take the exit for CA-156 West toward Monterey Peninsula. Continue onto CA-1 South, then use exit 402B for Del Monte Avenue towards Monterey.

GPS Coordinates: 36.6093125° N, 121.8953125° W

Best Time to Visit: Late spring to early fall for best weather and whale-watching opportunities.

Pass/Permit/Fees: No fees for most beach areas, parking fees may apply.

Did You Know? Monterey Bay is home to the world's largest marine sanctuary, protecting over 6,000 square miles of ocean.

Website: http://monterey.org/

Monterey Bay Aquarium

Dive into an underwater wonderland at the Monterey Bay Aquarium, situated on the historic Cannery Row. Renowned for its incredible marine exhibits, this top-tier aquarium offers interactive experiences that mesmerize visitors of all ages. Wander through immersive tanks showcasing the vibrant habitats of jellyfish, sea otters, and even deep-sea creatures. Don't miss the Open Sea exhibit, where you can watch schools of tuna and sharks glide past. The aquarium's commitment to marine conservation and education ensures an enriching visit every time.

Location: 886 Cannery Row, Monterey, CA 93940-1085

Closest City or Town: Monterey, California

How to Get There: From CA-1 South, take exit 402B for Del Monte Avenue toward Monterey. Continue on Cannery Row to reach the aquarium.

GPS Coordinates: 36.6182017° N, 121.9019479° W

Best Time to Visit: Year-round, with weekdays being less crowded.

Pass/Permit/Fees: Admission fees apply; check the website for current pricing.

Did You Know? The Monterey Bay Aquarium was the first to successfully exhibit a living kelp forest.

Website: http://montereybayaquarium.org/

MORRO BAY

Morro Rock

Admire the striking silhouette of Morro Rock, an ancient volcanic plug situated in Morro Bay, California. This iconic landmark serves as a dramatic natural backdrop for a host of outdoor activities. You can stroll along the beach, go birdwatching, or enjoy a picturesque picnic with the rock towering above. Sailors and kayakers often circle the base, offering unique vantage points of this geological wonder. Morro Rock is not just a stunning visual centerpiece; it is a sanctuary for a variety of seabirds and marine life.

Location: Coleman Dr, Morro Bay, CA 93442

Closest City or Town: Morro Bay, California

How to Get There: From US-101, take the exit for CA-1 South and follow signs to Morro Bay. Continue on Main Street to Coleman Drive.

GPS Coordinates: 35.3719101° N, 120.8646532° W

Best Time to Visit: Spring through fall for pleasant weather and clear views.

Pass/Permit/Fees: Free access; parking fees may apply.

Did You Know? Morro Rock is one of nine extinct volcanic peaks known as the Nine Sisters stretching from San Luis Obispo to Morro Bay.

Website: http://www.morro-bay.ca.us/index.aspx?NID=383

PALM DESERT

The Living Desert Zoo and Gardens

Step into a unique desert ecosystem at The Living Desert Zoo and Gardens, located in Palm Desert, California. This captivating zoo showcases the diverse flora and fauna of desert environments from around the world. You can wander through extensive cactus gardens, marvel at the desert wildlife, or even ride a camel. Educational exhibits and live demonstrations make this a perfect spot for families. The blend of arid landscapes and interactive experiences creates an enriching adventure in the heart of the desert.

Location: 47900 Portola Ave, Palm Desert, CA 92260, USA

Closest City or Town: Palm Desert, California

How to Get There: Take I-10 East towards Palm Desert. Exit at Washington Street and head south, then turn right onto Portola Avenue.

GPS Coordinates: 33.6999789° N, 116.3744166° W

Best Time to Visit: Fall through spring when temperatures are mild.

Pass/Permit/Fees: Admission fees apply; check the website for details.

Did You Know? The zoo's model train display is one of the largest in the world, covering over 3,300 square feet.

Website: http://www.livingdesert.org/

PALM SPRINGS

Indian Canyons

Experience the serene beauty of Indian Canyons, a stunning natural area located just south of Palm Springs, California. This pristine landscape offers an array of hiking trails winding through lush palm oases, striking rock formations, and tranquil streams. Explore the history and culture of the Agua Caliente Band of Cahuilla Indians who have lived in the area for centuries. The natural beauty combined with its rich cultural heritage makes Indian Canyons a must-visit for any adventurer.

Location: 38520 S Palm Canyon Dr, Palm Springs, CA 92264

Closest City or Town: Palm Springs, California

How to Get There: Take CA-111 South from downtown Palm Springs, then turn right onto S Palm Canyon Drive.

GPS Coordinates: 33.5020104° N, 117.6626909° W

Best Time to Visit: Fall to spring for comfortable hiking weather.

Pass/Permit/Fees: Entrance fee required; visit the website for detailed pricing.

Did You Know? Indian Canyons is home to the largest collection of California Fan Palms (Washingtonia filifera) in the world.

Website: http://indian-canyons.com//

Palm Springs Air Museum

Find your sense of adventure at the Palm Springs Air Museum, a captivating destination in Palm Springs, California. Here, visitors can explore an impressive collection of vintage aircraft from WWII, Korea, and Vietnam, meticulously maintained and displayed in hangars and open-air exhibits. The museum offers the chance to experience history through immersive displays and interactive exhibits. You can even climb aboard a bomber or witness a flight demonstration. Located in the heart of the Coachella Valley, it's a perfect stop for aviation enthusiasts and history buffs alike.

Location: 745 N Gene Autry Trl, Palm Springs, CA 92262-5464

Closest City or Town: Palm Springs, California

How to Get There: From downtown Palm Springs, take E Vista Chino east, turn left onto N Gene Autry Trail, and the museum will be on your left.

GPS Coordinates: 33.8351814° N, 116.5058606° W

Best Time to Visit: Spring and fall for comfortable temperatures

Pass/Permit/Fees: Admission fees apply; visit the website for pricing details.

Did You Know? The museum's collection includes over 70 aircraft, including the world's largest collection of flyable WWII aircraft.

Website: http://palmspringsairmuseum.org/

VillageFest

Immerse yourself in the vibrant atmosphere of Palm Springs VillageFest, a lively street fair held every Thursday evening. Located in downtown Palm Springs, this event transforms Palm Canyon Drive into a bustling marketplace filled with local vendors, artisans, and food stalls. You can browse handmade crafts, savor delicious street food, and enjoy live entertainment. The street comes alive with a mix of visitors and locals, creating a dynamic and festive ambiance perfect for a night out.

Location: 401 S Pavilion Way, Palm Springs, CA 92262

Closest City or Town: Palm Springs, California

How to Get There: From Interstate 10, take the CA-111 exit towards Palm Springs, then turn right onto S Pavilion Way.

GPS Coordinates: 33.8169830° N, 116.5252820° W

Best Time to Visit: Thursday evenings year-round

Pass/Permit/Fees: Free admission

Did You Know? VillageFest has been a beloved weekly tradition for over 25 years, attracting visitors from all over.

Website: https://www.facebook.com/PalmSpringsVillagefest/

PALO ALTO

Stanford University

Embark on an intellectual and architectural adventure at Stanford University, a prestigious academic institution located in Palo Alto, California. Founded in 1885 by Leland and Jane Stanford, the university is renowned for its research, innovation, and stunning campus. Visitors can stroll through the expansive grounds, visit the Cantor Arts Center, or see the iconic Hoover Tower. The university also offers beautiful gardens, historic buildings, and fascinating museums, making it a must-visit for anyone with a love for learning and exploration.

Location: 450 Serra Mall, Palo Alto, CA 94305-2004

Closest City or Town: Palo Alto, California

How to Get There: From US-101, take the Embarcadero Rd exit westbound to the university's main entrance.

GPS Coordinates: 37.4282641° N, 122.1688453° W

Best Time to Visit: Year-round, with spring and fall being particularly pleasant

Pass/Permit/Fees: Free access; some museums and exhibits may have separate fees.

Did You Know? Stanford's 8,180-acre campus is one of the largest in the United States and includes over 700 buildings.

Website: http://www.stanford.edu/

SACRAMENTO

California State Railroad Museum

Step back in time at the California State Railroad Museum in Sacramento, a fascinating destination dedicated to the history of railroads in California and the American West. Located in Old Sacramento, this museum showcases beautifully restored locomotives and railcars. Visitors can learn about the Transcontinental Railroad, explore themed exhibits, and even take a ride on a historic train. It's an exhilarating experience for families, train enthusiasts, and history lovers alike.

Location: 125 I St, Sacramento, CA 95814-2204

Closest City or Town: Sacramento, California

How to Get There: From I-5, take the J Street exit and follow signs to Old Sacramento.

GPS Coordinates: 38.5849368° N, 121.5043016° W

Best Time to Visit: Year-round

Pass/Permit/Fees: Admission fees apply; check the website for details.

Did You Know? The museum is home to over 225,000 square feet of exhibits dedicated to the history of the American railroad.

Website: http://www.californiarailroad.museum/

Old Sacramento

Discover the charm and history of Old Sacramento, a 28-acre National Historic Landmark District situated along the Sacramento River. This vibrant area offers a glimpse into California's Gold Rush era with its preserved buildings, wooden sidewalks, and cobblestone streets. Visitors can explore museums, dine at historic eateries, shop at unique boutiques, and take riverboat cruises. It's a delightful blend of history and modern attractions, making it a perfect destination for anyone wanting to experience the old and new of Sacramento.

CALIFORNIA BUCKET LIST

Location: 1014 2nd St, Sacramento, CA 95814-3202

Closest City or Town: Sacramento, California

How to Get There: From I-5, take the J Street exit and follow signs to Old Sacramento.

GPS Coordinates: 38.5827373° N, 121.5046528° W

Best Time to Visit: Spring and fall for pleasant weather

Pass/Permit/Fees: Free to enter; individual attractions may require fees.

Did You Know? Old Sacramento was developed during the California Gold Rush and remains a cornerstone of the city's heritage.

Website: http://oldsacramento.com/

SAN DIEGO

Birch Aquarium at Scripps

Dive into the wonders of the ocean at Birch Aquarium at Scripps, a marine sanctuary located in La Jolla, San Diego, California. Discover the mysteries of marine life through interactive exhibits and stunning displays of colorful coral reefs and fascinating sea creatures. You can explore the educational tide pools, watch captivating live feedings, and engage in hands-on activities that entertain and educate visitors of all ages. Nestled atop a hill with breathtaking views of the Pacific Ocean, Birch Aquarium serves as the public outreach center for the renowned Scripps Institution of Oceanography.

Location: 2300 Expedition Way Scripps Institute, La Jolla, San Diego, CA 92037

Closest City or Town: La Jolla, San Diego, California

How to Get There: From I-5, take La Jolla Village Drive exit, head west, then turn right on Expedition Way.

GPS Coordinates: 32.8658136° N, 117.2506390° W

Best Time to Visit: Year-round, with fewer crowds on weekdays.

Pass/Permit/Fees: General admission fees apply; visit the website for detailed pricing.

Did You Know? The Birch Aquarium at Scripps features more than 60 habitats showcasing the diverse marine life of the Pacific.

Website: http://www.aquarium.ucsd.edu/

Cabrillo National Monument

Immerse yourself in a blend of history and natural beauty at Cabrillo National Monument, situated at the southern tip of the Point Loma Peninsula in San Diego, California. This historic park commemorates the landing of Juan Rodríguez Cabrillo in 1542, the first European to set foot on the West Coast of the United States. You can explore the monument, visit the Old Point Loma Lighthouse, and hike scenic trails that offer panoramic views of the San Diego Bay and the Pacific

Ocean. This location also provides an excellent spot for whale watching during migration seasons.

Location: 1800 Cabrillo Memorial Dr, San Diego, CA 92106

Closest City or Town: San Diego, California

How to Get There: From downtown San Diego, take Harbor Drive to Canon Street, then follow signs to Cabrillo National Monument.

GPS Coordinates: 32.6742027° N, 117.2394643° W

Best Time to Visit: Spring and fall for mild weather and clear views.

Pass/Permit/Fees: Entrance fees apply; visit the website for current rates.

Did You Know? Cabrillo National Monument offers one of the best vantage points in San Diego for viewing the annual whale migration.

Website: http://www.nps.gov/cabr

Coronado Bridge

Cross over a marvel of engineering at the Coronado Bridge, which elegantly spans the San Diego Bay, linking San Diego with Coronado Island. This iconic bridge, renowned for its distinctive curved design and striking blue color, offers drivers breathtaking views of the bay and the city skyline. Approximately two miles long and rising to a height of 200 feet, it allows for the passage of naval ships below. Enjoy the ride as you head to the beautiful beaches, historic sites, and charming shopping areas of Coronado Island.

Location: State Route 75 South Embarcadero, San Diego, CA 92101

Closest City or Town: San Diego, California

How to Get There: Access the bridge from Interstate 5 South in downtown San Diego, following signs for State Route 75.

GPS Coordinates: 32.6894411° N, 117.1533503° W

Best Time to Visit: Year-round for stunning vistas and smooth traffic.

Pass/Permit/Fees: Free to cross.

Did You Know? The Coronado Bridge was inaugurated in 1969 and received an award for its structural design.

Website:
http://www.dot.ca.gov/hq/esc/tollbridge/Coronado/Corofacts.ht
ml

La Jolla Cove

Explore the natural beauty of La Jolla Cove, a stunning beach nestled in a picturesque cove in La Jolla, San Diego, California. Famous for its clear waters and vibrant marine life, it's an ideal spot for snorkeling, diving, and kayaking. Situated within the San Diego-La Jolla Underwater Park, this protected area is home to colorful Garibaldi fish, leopard sharks, and sea lions. Visitors can also enjoy a scenic beachfront walk, relax on the sandy shores, and take in breathtaking sunset views.

Location: 1100 Coast Blvd, La Jolla, San Diego, CA 92037-3600

Closest City or Town: La Jolla, San Diego, California

How to Get There: From I-5, exit on La Jolla Parkway, turn right onto Prospect Street, then left onto Coast Blvd.

GPS Coordinates: 32.8503526° N, 117.2730412° W

Best Time to Visit: Summer and early fall for warm water temperatures.

Pass/Permit/Fees: Free access.

Did You Know? La Jolla Cove is part of the protected underwater Ecological Reserve, making fishing and removing marine life illegal.

Website: https://en.wikipedia.org/wiki/La_Jolla

La Jolla Shores Park

Embrace the laid-back beach lifestyle at La Jolla Shores Park, a popular recreational spot in La Jolla, San Diego, California. Known for its wide sandy beach and gentle surf, it's perfect for swimming, sunbathing, and picnicking. This family-friendly park also offers ample opportunities for kayaking, paddleboarding, and beach volleyball. With its inviting atmosphere and stunning coastal views, it's an excellent destination for both relaxation and adventure.

Location: 8300 Camino del Oro, La Jolla, San Diego, CA 92037

Closest City or Town: La Jolla, San Diego, California

How to Get There: From I-5, take the La Jolla Parkway exit, then turn right onto Camino del Oro.

GPS Coordinates: 32.8581537° N, 117.2561029° W

Best Time to Visit: Summer for ideal beach weather.

Pass/Permit/Fees: Free access.

Did You Know? La Jolla Shores Park is adjacent to the Scripps Institution of Oceanography, which is one of the oldest and most important centers for ocean and Earth science research in the world.

Website: https://www.sandiego.gov/lifeguards/beaches/shores/

Little Italy

Savor the flavors and charm in Little Italy, a vibrant neighborhood nestled in San Diego, California. This historic area invites visitors to explore its bustling streets filled with authentic Italian eateries, trendy boutiques, and lively piazzas. Indulge in a pasta dish at a local trattoria, sip an espresso at an outdoor café, or immerse yourself in the culture at the weekly farmers' market. Each visit promises a delightful blend of culinary delights and rich cultural heritage, making it a must-visit destination.

Location: 2008 India St, San Diego, CA 92101

Closest City or Town: San Diego, California

How to Get There: From I-5, take the Front St/Civic Center exit and follow signs to Little Italy.

GPS Coordinates: 32.7256430° N, 117.1693786° W

Best Time to Visit: Year-round, but spring and fall offer mild weather and vibrant outdoor events.

Pass/Permit/Fees: Free to enter, individual dining and shopping costs vary.

Did You Know? Little Italy hosts the annual Festa! celebration, the largest Italian cultural festival on the West Coast.

Website: http://www.littleitalysd.com/

Mission Beach

Dive into the fun at Mission Beach, a bustling boardwalk and beach community in San Diego, California. Stretching along the Pacific Ocean, Mission Beach offers golden sands, surf-ready waves, and a classic California beach vibe. You can take a spin on the historic Giant Dipper roller coaster at Belmont Park, enjoy a bike ride down the boardwalk, or just relax in the sun. It's the perfect spot for beach-goers, thrill-seekers, and anyone looking to soak up the sun.

Location: 3200 Ocean Front Walk Surfrider Square, San Diego, CA 92109

Closest City or Town: San Diego, California

How to Get There: From I-5, take Garnet Ave/Mission Bay Dr exit, head west on Garnet Ave, and follow signs to Mission Beach.

GPS Coordinates: 32.7716617° N, 117.2527833° W

Best Time to Visit: Late spring through early fall for the best beach weather.

Pass/Permit/Fees: Free beach access, parking fees may apply.

Did You Know? The Belmont Park amusement park with the Giant Dipper roller coaster has been thrilling visitors since 1925.

Website: https://en.wikipedia.org/wiki/Mission_Beach,_San_Diego

Mt. Soledad National Veterans Memorial

Honor the nation's heroes at Mt. Soledad National Veterans Memorial in La Jolla, San Diego, California. Perched atop Mount Soledad, this memorial offers breathtaking 360-degree views of San Diego and the Pacific Ocean. Wander through plaques commemorating veterans from all branches of the military, paying tribute to their service and sacrifice. It's a serene and inspiring place, perfect for reflection and appreciation of history.

Location: 6905 La Jolla Scenic Drive South, La Jolla, San Diego, CA 92037

Closest City or Town: La Jolla, San Diego, California

How to Get There: From I-5, take La Jolla Pkwy exit, drive west onto La Jolla Scenic Drive South, and follow signs to the memorial.

GPS Coordinates: 32.8395636° N, 117.2428411° W

Best Time to Visit: Year-round, with clear days offering the most stunning views.

Pass/Permit/Fees: Free to visit, donations accepted.

Did You Know? The memorial is one of the few in the nation that honors veterans, living and deceased, from the Revolutionary War to present day.

Website: http://soledadmemorial.org/

Old Town San Diego

Step into the past at Old Town San Diego, the birthplace of California. Located in San Diego, this vibrant area re-creates life as it was in the 19th century. Wander through historic buildings, visit museums, and enjoy lively music and dance performances. You can also indulge in delicious Mexican cuisine at the town's many restaurants. It's a charming destination offering a rich blend of history, culture, and fun.

Location: 4426101600, San Diego, CA 92110

Closest City or Town: San Diego, California

How to Get There: From I-5, take the Old Town Ave exit and follow signs to the historical district.

GPS Coordinates: 32.7542167° N, 117.1969793° W

Best Time to Visit: Year-round, with special events held throughout the year.

Pass/Permit/Fees: Free to enter, individual attraction fees may vary.

Did You Know? Old Town San Diego is often considered the first European settlement in what is now California, dating back to 1769.

Website: http://oldtownsandiegoguide.com/

Old Town San Diego State Historic Park

Travel back in time at Old Town San Diego State Historic Park, a lively testament to California's early days. Situated in San Diego, the park preserves and recreates the feel of the 1800s with historical buildings, museums, and costumed interpreters. You can explore the old adobe homes, shop for unique souvenirs, or dine in historic settings. It's a rich cultural experience that brings history alive for all ages.

Location: 4002 Wallace St, San Diego, CA 92110

Closest City or Town: San Diego, California

How to Get There: From I-5, take the Old Town Ave exit, and follow signs to the state historic park.

GPS Coordinates: 32.7549063° N, 117.1976407° W

Best Time to Visit: Year-round, particularly lively during special historical reenactments.

Pass/Permit/Fees: Free to enter, some individual exhibits may have fees.

Did You Know? Old Town San Diego State Historic Park is one of California's most visited state parks, drawing over six million visitors annually.

Website: https://www.facebook.com/oldtownsandiego/

Petco Park

Cheer on the San Diego Padres at Petco Park, a premier destination for baseball fans. Situated in downtown San Diego, this state-of-the-art stadium offers an incredible game-day experience with stunning views of the city skyline and San Diego Bay. You can enjoy the electric atmosphere, explore unique food vendors, and catch a home run in the outfield park. The venue also hosts concerts and events, making it a year-round attraction for sports enthusiasts and concert-goers alike.

Location: 100 Park Blvd, San Diego, CA 92101-7405

Closest City or Town: San Diego, California

How to Get There: From Interstate 5, take exit 15B for Sixth Avenue and follow signs to Park Boulevard.

GPS Coordinates: 32.7070275° N, 117.1548988° W

Best Time to Visit: Throughout the MLB season, from April to October.

Pass/Permit/Fees: Varying ticket prices depending on the event; visit the website for details.

Did You Know? Petco Park features a "Park at the Park" area with a grassy hill where fans can lounge and watch the game.

Website: http://www.mlb.com/padres

Point Loma

Discover the captivating Point Loma, a scenic peninsula that offers breathtaking views of San Diego Bay and the Pacific Ocean. This historical site marks the landing point of the first European expedition to what is now California. Visitors can explore the Cabrillo National Monument, historic Old Point Loma Lighthouse, and tide pools teeming with marine life. The striking cliffs and the serene coastal environment make it an ideal spot for hiking, bird watching, and photography.

Location: 1800 Cabrillo Memorial Dr, San Diego, CA 92106

Closest City or Town: San Diego, California

How to Get There: From downtown San Diego, follow N Harbor Drive to Rosecrans Street, then follow signs to Cabrillo National Monument.

GPS Coordinates: 32.6747076° N, 117.2395300° W

Best Time to Visit: Spring and Fall for mild weather and clear skies.

Pass/Permit/Fees: Entrance fees apply; visit the website for details.

Did You Know? Point Loma is one of the best places in San Diego for whale-watching during migration seasons.

Website:
https://www.sandiego.gov/citycouncil/cd2/communities/pointloma

San Diego Zoo

Immerse yourself in the wonders of the animal kingdom at the world-renowned San Diego Zoo. Located in Balboa Park, this expansive zoo houses over 3,500 animals representing more than 650 species. You can wander through themed habitats, embark on a guided bus tour, or catch the aerial tram for aerial views of the exhibits. Don't miss the Giant Panda Research Station, home to adorable pandas, or the lush Elephant Odyssey habitat.

Location: 2929 Zoo Drive Balboa Park, San Diego, CA 92101

Closest City or Town: San Diego, California

How to Get There: Take Park Boulevard to Zoo Place, following signs to the San Diego Zoo.

GPS Coordinates: 32.7360353° N, 117.1509849° W

Best Time to Visit: Year-round, with fewer crowds in the fall and winter.

Pass/Permit/Fees: General admission fees apply; refer to the website for current pricing.

Did You Know? The San Diego Zoo pioneered the concept of open-air, cageless exhibits that simulate natural animal habitats.

Website: http://zoo.sandiegozoo.org/

Seaport Village

Enjoy a relaxed waterfront experience at Seaport Village, a charming shopping and dining complex in the heart of Downtown San Diego. Set along the picturesque San Diego Bay, this bustling area features quaint shops, diverse eateries, and live entertainment. Visitors can stroll along the boardwalk, ride the historic carousel, and experience the vibrant ambiance of this coastal destination.

Location: 849 W Harbor Dr, Downtown, San Diego, CA 92101-7744

Closest City or Town: San Diego, California

How to Get There: From Interstate 5, take the Front Street exit and follow signs to Seaport Village.

GPS Coordinates: 32.7090645° N, 117.1709366° W

Best Time to Visit: Year-round, with weekends offering a lively atmosphere.

Pass/Permit/Fees: Free access; individual shops and dining prices vary.

Did You Know? Seaport Village hosts an annual Busker Festival, featuring street performers from around the world.

Website: https://www.facebook.com/SeaportVillage/

SeaWorld

Dive into adventure and marine wonder at SeaWorld San Diego, known for its thrilling rides, interactive exhibits, and mesmerizing animal shows. Located in Mission Bay, this theme park lets you explore marine life up close, ranging from playful dolphins to majestic killer whales. Enjoy adrenaline-pumping attractions like the Manta roller coaster or embark on a serene underwater journey at the Turtle Reef.

Location: 500 Sea World Drive, San Diego, CA 92109

Closest City or Town: San Diego, California

How to Get There: From Interstate 5, take exit 21 for Sea World Drive and follow signs to the park.

GPS Coordinates: 32.7642958° N, 117.2264396° W

Best Time to Visit: Spring and fall for mild weather and fewer crowds.

Pass/Permit/Fees: Admission fees apply; visit the website for ticket information.

Did You Know? SeaWorld San Diego operates one of the largest marine mammal rescue programs in the world.

Website: http://seaworld.com/san-diego/

Sunset Cliffs Natural Park

Uncover the striking beauty of Sunset Cliffs Natural Park, a coastal wonderland in San Diego, California. Dramatically perched along the Pacific Ocean, this park offers breathtaking cliffside views, ideal for sunsets that paint the sky in brilliant hues. Hike the scenic trails, explore tide pools teeming with marine life, and witness waves crashing against the rugged cliffs. Unique geological formations and stunning ocean vistas make this location perfect for photographers, nature lovers, and anyone seeking solace by the sea.

Location: Ladera St, San Diego, CA 92107-4015

Closest City or Town: San Diego, California

How to Get There: From I-5 South, take the interstate 8 West, exit at Sunset Cliffs Blvd; follow signs to the park.

GPS Coordinates: 32.7194530° N, 117.2556285° W

Best Time to Visit: Year-round, with evenings offering the most spectacular sunsets.

Pass/Permit/Fees: Free access

Did You Know? Sunset Cliffs is known for sea caves, making it a popular spot for adventurous explorers.

Website: http://www.sandiego.gov/park-and-recreation/parks/regional/shoreline/sunset/

Torrey Pines State Natural Reserve

Discover the natural wonder of Torrey Pines State Natural Reserve in San Diego, California. This stunning coastal reserve is dedicated to preserving the rare and beautiful Torrey pine trees. Engage in activities like hiking trails offering cliffside views of the Pacific, spotting wildlife in its natural habitat, and basking in the serene, untouched beauty of Southern California's coastline. A haven for outdoor enthusiasts and adventurers alike, its unique features include dramatic sandstone formations and breathtaking ocean vistas.

Location: 12600 N Torrey Pines Rd, San Diego, CA 92037

Closest City or Town: San Diego, California

How to Get There: From I-5, exit at Carmel Valley Road, head west and turn left onto North Torrey Pines Road; the entrance will be on your right.

GPS Coordinates: 32.9209345° N, 117.2514443° W

Best Time to Visit: Spring and fall for mild weather

Pass/Permit/Fees: Day-use fee applies; for more details, check the website.

Did You Know? The Torrey pine is one of the rarest pine species in the world, found only in this reserve and on Santa Rosa Island.

Website: https://torreypine.org/

USS Midway Museum

Step aboard the legendary USS Midway Museum in San Diego, California, and immerse yourself in naval aviation history. Located along the city's picturesque harbor, this retired aircraft carrier offers a hands-on experience with restored aircraft, flight simulators, and guided tours by veterans. Explore the engine room, the captain's quarters, and the expansive flight deck. The museum's interactive exhibits and impressive collection of historic planes capture the imagination of visitors of all ages.

Location: 910 N Harbor Drive, San Diego, CA 92101-5811

Closest City or Town: San Diego, California

How to Get There: From I-5, take the Front Street exit, continue on W Ash Street, and turn left on N Harbor Drive.

GPS Coordinates: 32.7137398° N, 117.1751265° W

Best Time to Visit: Year-round, with weekdays less crowded.

Pass/Permit/Fees: Admission fees apply; for specific pricing, see the website.

Did You Know? The USS Midway was the longest-serving aircraft carrier in the 20th century, active from 1945 to 1992.

Website: http://www.midway.org/

SAN FRANCISCO

Alcatraz Island

Venture into the mysterious past at Alcatraz Island, located in the San Francisco Bay, California. Once a notorious federal penitentiary, this island now serves as a fascinating historical site. Explore the infamous cell blocks, learn about legendary inmates, and enjoy panoramic views of the San Francisco skyline. Accessible via a scenic ferry ride, Alcatraz offers guided tours that bring its intriguing history and dramatic tales of escape attempts to life.

Location: 31 San Francisco Pier 33 Alcatraz Island, San Francisco, CA 94124

Closest City or Town: San Francisco, California

How to Get There: From downtown San Francisco, head to Pier 33 for the Alcatraz ferry; bookings recommended.

GPS Coordinates: 37.8065008° N, 122.4045279° W

Best Time to Visit: Spring and fall for crisp weather

Pass/Permit/Fees: Ferry and tour fees apply; book tickets in advance.

Did You Know? Alcatraz Island was also a 19th-century military fort before becoming a federal prison in 1934.

Website: https://www.cityexperiences.com/san-francisco/city-cruises/alcatraz/?utm_source=google&utm_medium=organic&utm_campaign=alcatraz-city-cruises-google-listing

Aquarium of the Bay

Get up close with marine life at the Aquarium of the Bay, located at the iconic Fisherman's Wharf in San Francisco, California. This captivating aquarium showcases the diverse marine ecosystems of San Francisco Bay. Wander through tunnels surrounded by fish, see playful sea otters, and engage in interactive touch pools. It's an educational and enchanting experience for families and wildlife enthusiasts alike, offering a window into the underwater world of Northern California.

Location: Embarcadero & Beach St Pier 39, San Francisco, CA 94133

Closest City or Town: San Francisco, California

How to Get There: From downtown San Francisco, head north on Embarcadero to Pier 39.

GPS Coordinates: 37.8086487° N, 122.4093299° W

Best Time to Visit: Year-round, with weekdays less crowded

Pass/Permit/Fees: Admission fees apply; visit the website for details.

Did You Know? The Aquarium of the Bay features over 20,000 marine animals, including shark species native to the bay.

Website: http://www.aquariumofthebay.org/

Asian Art Museum

Find your sense of wonder at the Asian Art Museum, a cultural treasure located in San Francisco, California. This captivating museum immerses visitors in a vast collection of Asian art, spanning ancient times to contemporary works. You can marvel at intricate ceramics, awe-inspiring sculptures, and delicate textiles that narrate the rich histories and cultures of Asia. Located in the heart of Civic Center, it provides an enlightening exploration of the artistic achievements of diverse Asian civilizations.

Location: 200 Larkin St, San Francisco, CA 94102-4734

Closest City or Town: San Francisco, California

How to Get There: From US-101, take the Van Ness Avenue exit and head toward Larkin St.

GPS Coordinates: 37.779567° N, 122.416090° W

Best Time to Visit: Year-round, with fewer crowds on weekdays

Pass/Permit/Fees: Admission fees apply; visit the website for details

Did You Know? The Asian Art Museum holds one of the most comprehensive collections of Asian art in the world, with over 18,000 objects.

Website: http://www.asianart.org/

Cable Car Museum

Revel in a slice of San Francisco history at the Cable Car Museum. Located in the Nob Hill neighborhood, this unique museum offers an insightful look into the iconic cable cars that have been a symbol of the city since the late 19th century. You can see the original cable car mechanisms in action, explore historic photographs and artifacts, and even step inside vintage cable cars. This museum provides a fascinating behind-the-scenes glimpse into one of San Francisco's most enduring traditions.

Location: 1201 Mason Street, San Francisco, CA 94108-1071

Closest City or Town: San Francisco, California

How to Get There: From US-101, take the exit toward Van Ness Avenue, then turn onto California Street and finally Mason Street.

GPS Coordinates: 37.7946366° N, 122.4115074° W

Best Time to Visit: Year-round, with fewer visitors in the morning

Pass/Permit/Fees: Free admission

Did You Know? The Cable Car Museum is also the central hub of San Francisco's cable car system, where you can see the giant wheels pulling the cables.

Website: http://www.cablecarmuseum.org/index.html

California Academy of Sciences

Immerse yourself in the wonders of nature and science at the California Academy of Sciences, located in the heart of San Francisco's Golden Gate Park. This state-of-the-art museum features a planetarium, a rainforest dome, an aquarium, and a natural history museum all under one roof. You can explore vibrant coral reefs, watch live penguin feedings, and even experience simulated earthquakes. This dynamic institution seamlessly blends education and entertainment, making it a must-visit for all ages.

Location: 55 Music Concourse Dr, Golden Gate Park, San Francisco, CA 94118-4503

Closest City or Town: San Francisco, California

How to Get There: From US-101, take the Fell Street exit, then continue to Stanyan Street and head into Golden Gate Park.

GPS Coordinates: 37.7698646° N, 122.4660947° W

Best Time to Visit: Anytime during the year, with weekdays less crowded

Pass/Permit/Fees: Admission fees apply; visit the website for specifics

Did You Know? The California Academy of Sciences is one of the largest natural history museums in the world, housing over 46 million specimens.

Website: http://www.calacademy.org/

Chinatown

Step into the vibrant culture of Chinatown, a bustling neighborhood in San Francisco. As the largest Chinatown outside of Asia, this area is steeped in rich history and cultural traditions. You can wander through colorful streets adorned with lanterns, visit traditional herbal shops, and dine on authentic Chinese cuisine. Located along Grant Avenue, it's a sensory feast of sights, sounds, and flavors that provides a glimpse into a unique part of San Francisco's heritage.

Location: Grant Avenue, San Francisco, CA 94108

Closest City or Town: San Francisco, California

How to Get There: From downtown San Francisco, take Grant Avenue northward.

GPS Coordinates: 37.7919766° N, 122.4058481° W

Best Time to Visit: Year-round, especially during the annual Chinese New Year celebrations

Pass/Permit/Fees: Free to explore

Did You Know? San Francisco's Chinatown was established in 1848 and is the oldest Chinatown in North America.

Website: https://en.wikipedia.org/wiki/Chinatown,_San_Francisco

Coit Tower

Experience panoramic views of San Francisco from Coit Tower, perched atop Telegraph Hill. This historic tower offers unparalleled vistas of the city and the bay, along with stunning interior murals depicting life in 1930s San Francisco. You can take an elevator to the top for breathtaking scenes or explore the surrounding Pioneer Park. Located in the heart of the city, Coit Tower is a testament to San Francisco's artistic heritage and natural beauty.

Location: 1 Telegraph Hill Blvd, San Francisco, CA 94133-3106

Closest City or Town: San Francisco, California

How to Get There: From downtown San Francisco, take Lombard Street to Telegraph Hill Boulevard.

GPS Coordinates: 37.8023740° N, 122.4058178° W

Best Time to Visit: Clear days during any season for the best views

Pass/Permit/Fees: Entrance fees apply; check the website for details

Did You Know? Coit Tower was funded by Lillie Hitchcock Coit's bequest to enhance the beauty of the city she loved.

Website: http://sfrecpark.org/destination/telegraph-hill-pioneer-park/coit-tower/

de Young Museum

Embark on an artistic adventure at the de Young Museum, nestled in the heart of Golden Gate Park in San Francisco, California. This world-class museum offers a dynamic collection of American art from the 17th through the 21st centuries, textiles, and international contemporary art. You can meander through its innovative architectural spaces, admire works from various periods and cultures, and gaze at the panoramic views of the city from the Hamon Tower observation deck. Engaging exhibits and special events make every visit a fresh and inspiring experience.

Location: 50 Hagiwara Tea Garden Dr, Golden Gate Park, San Francisco, CA 94118-4502

Closest City or Town: San Francisco, California

How to Get There: From downtown San Francisco, take the 5 Fulton Muni bus line or drive via Fulton St and follow signs to Golden Gate Park.

GPS Coordinates: 37.7714690° N, 122.4686755° W

Best Time to Visit: Year-round, with weekdays being less crowded

Pass/Permit/Fees: Admission fees apply; visit the website for ticket prices.

Did You Know? The de Young Museum is built to withstand earthquakes, featuring a unique copper facade that will weather beautifully over time.

Website: http://deyoung.famsf.org/

Ferry Building Marketplace

Immerse yourself in culinary delights at the Ferry Building Marketplace, an iconic food hall and shopping center located on the San Francisco waterfront. This historic landmark invites visitors to savor artisanal foods, craft beverages, and boutique products from local vendors. Wander through the bustling market, sample fresh oysters, indulge in gourmet cheeses, and explore unique artisanal shops. The marketplace's vibrant atmosphere and stunning bay views make it a must-visit for food lovers and shoppers alike.

Location: 1 Ferry Building, The Embarcadero at Market Street, San Francisco, CA 94111-4209

Closest City or Town: San Francisco, California

How to Get There: From downtown San Francisco, take the Embarcadero Muni or BART to Embarcadero Station and walk to the Ferry Building.

GPS Coordinates: 37.7954425° N, 122.3936136° W

Best Time to Visit: Saturdays for the vibrant farmers market; weekdays for a more relaxed experience.

Pass/Permit/Fees: Free to enter, individual vendor prices vary.

Did You Know? The Ferry Building Marketplace opened in 1898 and was once the busiest transit terminal in the United States.

Website: http://www.ferrybuildingmarketplace.com/

Fisherman's Wharf

Find your seafaring spirit at Fisherman's Wharf, a historic and lively waterfront neighborhood in San Francisco, California. This vibrant area teems with seafood restaurants, souvenir shops, and street performers. Stroll along the famous Pier 39, watch sea lions basking in the sun, or embark on a scenic boat tour of the bay. With its rich maritime history and family-friendly activities, Fisherman's Wharf offers a quintessential San Francisco experience.

Location: Jefferson Street Between Hyde and Powell Streets, San Francisco, CA 94133

Closest City or Town: San Francisco, California

How to Get There: From downtown San Francisco, take the F-Market & Wharves streetcar to Fisherman's Wharf.

GPS Coordinates: 37.8068681° N, 122.4209381° W

Best Time to Visit: Summer and early fall for pleasant weather and lively events.

Pass/Permit/Fees: Free to explore the area; individual attractions have varying fees.

Did You Know? Fisherman's Wharf was the starting point for many fishing expeditions during the California Gold Rush.

Website: http://www.visitfishermanswharf.com/

Ghirardelli Square

Delight your senses at Ghirardelli Square, a charming historic landmark and shopping center in San Francisco, California. Originally a chocolate factory, this square now features upscale shops, restaurants, and the famous Ghirardelli Ice Cream & Chocolate Shop. Enjoy a delicious sundae, browse specialty stores, and take in views of the bay. Its blend of heritage and modern luxury makes Ghirardelli Square a sweet spot for visitors.

Location: 900 North Point St, At Polk Street, San Francisco, CA 94109-1197

Closest City or Town: San Francisco, California

How to Get There: From downtown San Francisco, ride the Powell-Hyde Cable Car to the stop at Ghirardelli Square.

GPS Coordinates: 37.8055225° N, 122.4226730° W

Best Time to Visit: Year-round, with evenings offering a cozy atmosphere.

Pass/Permit/Fees: Free to enter; individual store prices vary.

Did You Know? Ghirardelli Square was placed on the National Register of Historic Places in 1982.

Website: http://www.ghirardellisq.com/

Golden Gate Bridge

Marvel at the engineering masterpiece that is the Golden Gate Bridge, spanning the San Francisco Bay between San Francisco and Marin County. This iconic red-orange suspension bridge invites visitors to walk, bike, or drive across its expanse, offering panoramic views of the bay and the city skyline. Capture stunning photos, learn about its history at the visitor center, and experience the majesty of one of the world's most recognized landmarks.

Location: RG9C+XH, Presidio of San Francisco, San Francisco, California

Closest City or Town: San Francisco, California

How to Get There: From downtown San Francisco, head north on US-101 and follow signs to the Golden Gate Bridge.

GPS Coordinates: 37.8199375° N, 122.4785625° W

Best Time to Visit: Early mornings or late afternoons to avoid crowds and catch the best light for photography.

Pass/Permit/Fees: Free to walk or bike; toll fees apply for vehicles.

Did You Know? The Golden Gate Bridge's art deco design was a groundbreaking feat of engineering when it opened in 1937.

Website: https://www.goldengate.org/

Golden Gate Park

Find your sense of adventure and tranquility in Golden Gate Park, a sprawling urban escape in the heart of San Francisco, California. This vast green oasis spans over 1,000 acres, offering visitors an array of outdoor activities and scenic spots to explore.

Located at 501 Stanyan St, San Francisco, CA 94117-1898, the park is a treasure trove of attractions such as the renowned Japanese Tea Garden, the serene Stow Lake, and an array of sports fields and picnic areas.

You can stroll through vibrant botanical gardens, visit diverse museums, and even spot bison in the park's paddocks. Unique features include the impressive Conservatory of Flowers and the tranquil Shakespeare Garden, perfect for a reflective walk.

Soak up the sun, paddleboat on a serene lake, or simply relax in one of the many picturesque meadows.

Location: 501 Stanyan St, San Francisco, CA 94117-1898

Closest City or Town: San Francisco, California

How to Get There: Accessible from major roads, including Fell St and Lincoln Way, with multiple entrances across its expanse.

GPS Coordinates: 37.7718462° N, 122.4548329° W

Best Time to Visit: Year-round, with spring and fall offering the best weather.

Pass/Permit/Fees: Mostly free; some attractions may charge separate admission.

Did You Know? Golden Gate Park is larger than New York's Central Park and attracts over 24 million visitors each year.

Website: http://sfrecpark.org/destination/golden-gate-park/

Japanese Tea Garden

Transport yourself to a serene Japanese oasis at the Japanese Tea Garden, located within San Francisco's Golden Gate Park. This historic garden, the oldest public Japanese garden in the United States, offers visitors a tranquil escape with beautifully landscaped paths, koi ponds, and tea houses.

Found at 75 Hagiwara Tea Garden Drive, Golden Gate Park, San Francisco, CA 94118-4502, the garden was originally created as an exhibit for the 1894 California Midwinter International Exposition.

You can stroll through five acres of meticulously maintained gardens, sip traditional Japanese tea, and marvel at the iconic Drum Bridge and pagodas. This peaceful retreat is adorned with bonsai trees, flowering cherry blossoms, and an alluring Zen garden.

Enjoy an authentic experience by participating in a traditional tea ceremony while soaking in the beauty of Japanese horticultural artistry.

Location: 75 Hagiwara Tea Garden Drive, Golden Gate Park, San Francisco, CA 94118-4502

Closest City or Town: San Francisco, California

How to Get There: Access via John F Kennedy Drive inside Golden Gate Park, near the de Young Museum.

GPS Coordinates: 37.7700913° N, 122.4704359° W

Best Time to Visit: Spring for cherry blossoms; morning hours for a quieter experience.

Pass/Permit/Fees: Admission fees vary; check the website for details.

Did You Know? The garden's main gate, gift shop, and other structures were crafted by Japanese artisans using traditional techniques.

Website: http://sfjapaneseteagarden.org/

Lands End

Experience the rugged beauty of Lands End, a windswept coastal trail located at the edge of San Francisco, California. Known for its jaw-dropping vistas of the Pacific Ocean and historic shipwrecks, this destination promises both adventure and tranquility.

You can find this scenic wonder at El Camino del Mar Point Lobos Avenue, San Francisco, CA 94121, where the path meanders through cypress groves and along dramatic cliffsides offering spectacular views of the Golden Gate Bridge.

Hike along the Lands End Trail, explore the Sutro Baths ruins, and discover hidden beaches and tide pools. Unique features include the labyrinth at Eagle's Point and remnants of the historic railroad.

Perfect for hikers, photographers, and history buffs, Lands End captures the wild essence of San Francisco's coastline.

Location: El Camino del Mar Point Lobos Avenue, San Francisco, CA 94121

Closest City or Town: San Francisco, California

How to Get There: Accessible via Geary Blvd, traveling west to Great Highway, then follow signs to Point Lobos Avenue.

GPS Coordinates: 37.7797230° N, 122.5115887° W

Best Time to Visit: Year-round; clear days offer unbeatable views.

Pass/Permit/Fees: Free access.

Did You Know? Lands End offers breathtaking views of the Marin Headlands and the Pacific, making it a favorite spot for sunset watchers.

Website: https://www.parksconservancy.org/projects/lands-end-lookout

Legion of Honor

Delve into the world of art and history at the Legion of Honor, a prominent museum in San Francisco's Lincoln Park. This architectural gem houses an impressive collection of European paintings, sculptures, and decorative arts.
Situated at 100 34th Ave, Lincoln Park, San Francisco, CA 94121-1677, it was generously gifted by philanthropists Alma and Adolph Spreckels as a tribute to the Californian soldiers who perished in World War I.
Visitors can admire works by Rodin, Rembrandt, and Monet, and take in the striking neoclassical architecture. The museum's location atop a hill provides panoramic views of the Golden Gate Bridge and the surrounding bay.
Stroll through the sculpture garden, explore rotating exhibits, and enjoy a moment of contemplation in the serene setting.

Location: 100 34th Ave, Lincoln Park, San Francisco, CA 94121-1677

Closest City or Town: San Francisco, California

How to Get There: Take the 34th Ave exit from Clement St, and head north until you reach the museum.

GPS Coordinates: 37.7845037° N, 122.5008374° W

Best Time to Visit: Year-round; mornings for a quieter visit.

Pass/Permit/Fees: Admission fees apply; check the website for specific pricing.

Did You Know? The museum houses Auguste Rodin's The Thinker, one of the most iconic sculptures worldwide.

Website: http://legionofhonor.famsf.org/

Lombard Street

Experience the quirky charm of Lombard Street, the famous "crooked" street of San Francisco. Winding down Russian Hill, this iconic street is celebrated for its eight sharp turns and beautifully landscaped gardens.

Located at Lombard Street, The Presidio east to The Embarcadero, San Francisco, CA 94109, Lombard Street offers drivers and pedestrians a unique journey through one of the city's most visually striking areas.

You can drive down the sinuous road, photograph its whimsical curves, and enjoy panoramic views of the city and the bay. Unique features include vibrant flowerbeds lining the street and classic San Francisco architecture.

Whether you walk or drive, experiencing Lombard Street is a must-do for anyone visiting San Francisco.

Location: 2310 Hyde St #1, San Francisco, CA 94109

Closest City or Town: San Francisco, California

How to Get There: Accessible via Leavenworth St; the best approach is from the top at Hyde St.

GPS Coordinates: 37.8020146° N, 122.4195551° W

Best Time to Visit: Spring and summer when the flowers are in bloom.

Pass/Permit/Fees: Free access.

Did You Know? Lombard Street's sharp curves were designed to reduce the hill's natural 27% grade, making it safer for vehicles.

Website:
https://en.wikipedia.org/wiki/Lombard_Street_(San_Francisco)

Musee Mecanique

Step into a nostalgic journey through time at Musee Mecanique, an extraordinary museum packed with fascinating mechanical wonders. Situated on Pier 45 at the foot of Taylor Street in Fisherman's Wharf, San Francisco, this captivating museum houses one of the largest collections of coin-operated antique arcade machines and mechanical musical instruments in the world. You can engage with these vintage treasures, watch quirky automata come to life, and play old-fashioned games. Each machine has its own unique story, making it a playable history lesson and a delightful experience for all ages.

Location: Pier 45, Fishermen's Wharf foot of Taylor Street, San Francisco, CA 94133

Closest City or Town: San Francisco, California

How to Get There: From downtown San Francisco, head north on Embarcadero until you reach Taylor Street and follow signs for Fisherman's Wharf.

GPS Coordinates: 37.8093037° N, 122.4159684° W

Best Time to Visit: Year-round, with weekdays being quieter

Pass/Permit/Fees: Free entry, with individual costs for arcade machines

Did You Know? Musee Mecanique has over 300 mechanical machines, including one of the last remaining steam-powered motorcycles.

Website: http://www.museemecaniquesf.com/

Oracle Park

Catch the spirit of Major League Baseball at Oracle Park, home to the San Francisco Giants. Located on King Street in San Francisco, this state-of-the-art stadium is renowned for its exquisite views of the San Francisco Bay and its unique, fan-friendly features. You can enjoy a game while savoring local gourmet food, take a tour to explore behind the scenes, and even walk onto the field. Beyond baseball, the park hosts concerts and events, making it a bustling hub of activity throughout the year.

CALIFORNIA BUCKET LIST

Location: King Street, San Francisco, CA 94107-2134

Closest City or Town: San Francisco, California

How to Get There: From I-280, take the King Street exit, and follow signs to the ballpark.

GPS Coordinates: 37.7756700° N, 122.3951216° W

Best Time to Visit: During the MLB season, from April to October

Pass/Permit/Fees: Ticket prices vary depending on game and seating; check the website for details

Did You Know? Oracle Park features a giant Coca-Cola bottle with playground slides and a miniature baseball field known as The Little Giants Park.

Website: http://sfgiants.com/tours

Pier 39

Experience the festive ambiance of Pier 39, a vibrant waterfront destination in San Francisco. Located at the confluence of Beach Street and The Embarcadero, Pier 39 is buzzing with attractions, dining, shopping, and lively entertainment. You can watch the famous sea lions basking in the sun, enjoy breathtaking views of Alcatraz and the Golden Gate Bridge, and indulge in delicious seafood. This bustling pier offers a myriad of activities from carousel rides to street performances, making it a must-visit for families and tourists alike.

Location: Beach Street & The Embarcadero, San Francisco, CA 94133

Closest City or Town: San Francisco, California

How to Get There: Take the F-Market & Wharves streetcar to Pier 39 or drive along The Embarcadero.

GPS Coordinates: 37.8086730° N, 122.4098210° W

Best Time to Visit: Year-round, with summer offering the most vibrant atmosphere

Pass/Permit/Fees: Free to explore; individual attractions have fees.

Did You Know? Pier 39 is home to more than 50 specialty shops and 13 full-service restaurants, catering to every taste and interest.

Website: https://www.pier39.com//

Presidio of San Francisco

Find your sense of history and natural beauty at the Presidio of San Francisco, a former military post turned national park. Situated in the northwest corner of the city, this sprawling park offers a unique blend of historic sites, lush natural landscapes, and breathtaking vistas. You can explore military museums, hike scenic trails with views of the Golden Gate Bridge, and relax in the tranquil forests. The Presidio is a cultural and recreational haven perfect for history buffs, nature lovers, and outdoor enthusiasts.

Location: QGR8+98, Gibson Rd, San Francisco, CA 94129

Closest City or Town: San Francisco, California

How to Get There: Drive along Lombard Street to the Presidio entrance at any major gate; public transit options also available.

GPS Coordinates: 37.7905460° N, 122.4836409° W

Best Time to Visit: Spring and fall for mild weather

Pass/Permit/Fees: Free access; museum entries may have fees

Did You Know? The Presidio is home to the historic Lucasfilm headquarters, which features a life-sized Yoda fountain.

Website: http://www.presidio.gov/

San Francisco Bay

Embark on an adventurous exploration of the San Francisco Bay, the heart of the city's maritime culture. Located along the northern shoreline of the city, this vibrant body of water is framed by iconic landmarks such as the Golden Gate Bridge and Alcatraz Island. You can sail, kayak, or take a ferry trip across the bay, and enjoy waterfront parks, piers, and historic attractions that dot its shores. The bay offers an endless array of activities, from the excitement of sailing to the serenity of waterfront strolls.

Location: 999 Marine Dr, San Francisco, CA 94129

Closest City or Town: San Francisco, California

How to Get There: Accessible from numerous points throughout the city; Marine Drive is a popular starting spot.

GPS Coordinates: 37.8102547° N, 122.4765327° W

Best Time to Visit: Year-round, with summer offering the best conditions for water activities

Pass/Permit/Fees: Free to access; some activities and guided tours may have fees

Did You Know? The San Francisco Bay is one of the world's largest landlocked harbors and a renowned spot for sailing and yacht racing.

Website: http://baytrail.abag.ca.gov/

San Francisco Museum of Modern Art (SFMOMA)

Dive into the captivating world of contemporary art at the San Francisco Museum of Modern Art (SFMOMA). Located in the heart of San Francisco, this dynamic museum boasts an extensive collection of modern masterpieces and innovative exhibitions. Visitors can explore seven floors of brilliant artworks, ranging from paintings and sculptures to media installations. Unique features include site-specific works and the spacious Sculpture Garden. Join in on immersive experiences and admire pieces by renowned artists such as Warhol and Frida Kahlo.

Location: 151 3rd St Enter on Howard or Third Street, San Francisco, CA 94103-3107

Closest City or Town: San Francisco, California

How to Get There: From downtown San Francisco, head southeast on Market Street, turn right onto 3rd Street, and find SFMOMA on your right.

GPS Coordinates: 37.7857182° N, 122.4010508° W

Best Time to Visit: Weekdays to avoid large crowds.

Pass/Permit/Fees: Admission fees apply; visit the website for current pricing.

Did You Know? SFMOMA was the first museum on the west coast dedicated to modern and contemporary art.

Website: http://www.sfmoma.org/

Twin Peaks

Experience stunning panoramic views at Twin Peaks, San Francisco's famous vantage point. Located in the center of the city, these iconic hills offer unparalleled vistas of the Bay Area. You can drive, hike, or bike to the top, where the observation points provide 360-degree views. It's an ideal spot for photographers, nature lovers, and anyone looking to soak in the beauty of the cityscape. Unique features include the Sutro Tower landmark and native plant species along the trails.

Location: 501 Twin Peaks Blvd, San Francisco, CA 94114

Closest City or Town: San Francisco, California

How to Get There: From Market Street, turn onto Clayton Street and then Twin Peaks Boulevard.

GPS Coordinates: 37.7529149° N, 122.4474131° W

Best Time to Visit: Early morning or late afternoon for the best light and fewer crowds.

Pass/Permit/Fees: Free entry.

Did You Know? On clear days, visitors can spot up to seven Bay Area counties from the peaks.

Website: https://sfrecpark.org/facilities/facility/details/twin-peaks-384

Walt Disney Family Museum

Discover the magic and legacy of Walt Disney at the Walt Disney Family Museum, nestled in San Francisco's Presidio. This enchanting museum showcases the life and creativity of Disney through interactive exhibits, rare artifacts, and personal narrated tours. Visitors can marvel at original drawings, early animations, and the multiplane camera used in Disney's classic films. The museum encapsulates Disney's innovative spirit with engaging displays and breathtaking views of the Golden Gate Bridge.

Location: 104 Montgomery St The Presidio, San Francisco, CA 94129-1718

Closest City or Town: San Francisco, California

How to Get There: From downtown San Francisco, take Lombard Street to Van Ness Avenue, turn onto Bay Street, then follow signs to the Presidio.

GPS Coordinates: 37.8013783° N, 122.4586431° W

Best Time to Visit: Visit during weekdays or off-peak seasons for a more relaxed experience.

Pass/Permit/Fees: Admission fees apply; check the website for detailed pricing.

Did You Know? The museum was founded by Walt Disney's daughter and houses numerous awards Walt received during his lifetime.

Website: http://www.waltdisney.org/welcome-backSan Jose

Winchester Mystery House

Set off on a spine-tingling adventure at the Winchester Mystery House, a peculiar mansion in San Jose, California. Built by Sarah Winchester, the widow of the rifle magnate, this sprawling estate is famed for its architectural oddities, including staircases that lead nowhere and doors that open into walls. Visitors can embark on guided tours to explore the elaborate interiors and mysterious history. Unique features include the bizarre layouts of the rooms and the exquisite Victorian craftsmanship.

Location: 525 S Winchester Blvd North San Jose, San Jose, CA 95128-2588

Closest City or Town: San Jose, California

How to Get There: From I-280, take the Winchester Boulevard exit and travel north; the house will be on your right.

GPS Coordinates: 37.3183318° N, 121.9510491° W

Best Time to Visit: Fall for the special Halloween tours or any time during the year.

Pass/Permit/Fees: Admission fees apply; visit the website for tour prices.

Did You Know? The house contains approximately 160 rooms and construction continued for 38 years without ceasing.

Website: http://www.winchestermysteryhouse.com/

SAN JUAN CAPISTRANO

Mission San Juan Capistrano

Step into California's rich history at Mission San Juan Capistrano, located in San Juan Capistrano, California. Founded in 1776, this historic mission is known for its beautiful gardens, ornate chapel, and annual return of the swallows. Visitors can explore the centuries-old architecture, stroll through the serene grounds, and learn about the mission's role in California's early days. Unique features include the Great Stone Church ruins and the peaceful Serra Chapel.

Location: 26801 Old Mission Road, San Juan Capistrano, CA 92675

Closest City or Town: San Juan Capistrano, California

How to Get There: From I-5, take the exit onto Ortega Highway towards Mission San Juan Capistrano.

GPS Coordinates: 34.1382828° N, 118.3532976° W

Best Time to Visit: Spring for the return of the swallows or year-round.

Pass/Permit/Fees: Admission fees apply; check the website for more details.

Did You Know? The mission's bell wall is renowned for its significant role in alerting the community of events and emergencies.

Website: http://www.missionsjc.com/

SAN MARINO

The Huntington Library, Art Museum and Botanical Gardens

Discover a world of art, literature, and nature at The Huntington Library, Art Museum, and Botanical Gardens in San Marino, California. Stretching across 120 acres, this majestic estate boasts meticulously curated gardens, world-class art collections, and a vast library of rare manuscripts. You'll be captivated by the lush Japanese Garden, the serene Desert Garden, and the stunning European and American art on display. Whether you're a fan of horticulture, fine art, or history, this paradise offers something for everyone.

Location: 1151 Oxford Road, San Marino, CA 91108-1218

Closest City or Town: San Marino, California

How to Get There: From downtown Los Angeles, take I-110 North, then merge onto CA-134 East and exit at Orange Grove Blvd., continuing onto Sierra Madre Blvd. to Oxford Road.

GPS Coordinates: 34.1290452° N, 118.1145242° W

Best Time to Visit: Spring and fall offer mild weather for garden strolling.

Pass/Permit/Fees: Admission fees apply; check the website for accurate details.

Did You Know? The Huntington is home to the iconic Gutenberg Bible, one of the world's oldest and most valuable printed books.

Website: http://www.huntington.org/

SAN SIMEON

Hearst Castle

Immerse yourself in opulent grandeur at Hearst Castle, an architectural marvel perched on a hilltop in San Simeon, California. Created by media magnate William Randolph Hearst, this estate features lavish rooms, lush gardens, and a stunning collection of art and antiques. Wander through the opulent Neptune Pool, explore the opulent suites, or stroll through the vibrant gardens. Each visit offers a glimpse into the lavish lifestyle of the early 20th century elite.

Location: 750 Hearst Castle Road, San Simeon, CA 93452-9740

Closest City or Town: San Simeon, California

How to Get There: From US-1 in San Simeon, turn onto Hearst Castle Road and follow the signs to the visitor center.

GPS Coordinates: 35.6858301° N, 121.1681580° W

Best Time to Visit: Spring and fall for the most pleasant weather.

Pass/Permit/Fees: Admission fees vary by tour; check the website for ticket options.

Did You Know? Hearst Castle boasts an extensive collection of over 25,000 artifacts spanning millennia, many sourced from Mediterranean civilizations.

Website: http://hearstcastle.org/

SANTA BARBARA

Old Mission Santa Barbara

Step back in time at Old Mission Santa Barbara, also known as the "Queen of the Missions," a beautiful historical landmark in Santa Barbara, California. Founded in 1786 by Spanish Franciscans, this mission boasts exquisite architecture, tranquil gardens, and a rich history. Join a guided tour to explore the church, museum, and cemetery, or wander the lush gardens at your leisure. This iconic site illuminates the area's fascinating past and heritage.

Location: 2201 Laguna St, Santa Barbara, CA 93105-3611

Closest City or Town: Santa Barbara, California

How to Get There: From US-101, take the Mission Street exit and head east until you reach Laguna Street.

GPS Coordinates: 34.4384389° N, 119.7138382° W

Best Time to Visit: Spring and fall for perfect weather.

Pass/Permit/Fees: Admission fees apply; check the website for up-to-date prices.

Did You Know? The mission's iconic twin bell towers are unique among the California missions and a symbol of the city's heritage.

Website: http://www.santabarbaramission.org/

Santa Barbara County Courthouse

Marvel at the architectural splendor of the Santa Barbara County Courthouse in downtown Santa Barbara, California. This Spanish-Moorish style building is one of the most beautiful courthouses in the U.S., featuring lush gardens, hand-painted ceilings, and the iconic El Mirador clock tower. You can tour the courthouse, stroll through the scenic Sunken Garden, or enjoy panoramic views of the city and coastline from the tower.

Location: 1100 Anacapa St, Santa Barbara, CA 93101-2099

Closest City or Town: Santa Barbara, California

How to Get There: From US-101, take the Carrillo Street exit east, then turn left onto Anacapa Street.

GPS Coordinates: 34.4242013° N, 119.7023282° W

Best Time to Visit: Year-round with clear days offering the best views.

Pass/Permit/Fees: Free entry.

Did You Know? The courthouse's 85-foot Spirit of the Ocean fountain was carved from a single block of stone.

Website: https://www.sbcourthouse.org

State Street Underpass

Find your sense of urban discovery at the State Street Underpass in Santa Barbara, California. This pedestrian-friendly passageway is more than a means to cross beneath the bustling street—it's an artistic landmark adorned with murals and vibrant decorations. Connecting the downtown shopping district to the waterfront, it's the perfect spot to experience the local art scene while exploring the city.

Location: State Street W. Quinto St., Santa Barbara, CA 93117

Closest City or Town: Santa Barbara, California

How to Get There: From US-101, take the Castillo Street exit and head south to State Street.

GPS Coordinates: 34.4354353° N, 119.7210530° W

Best Time to Visit: Year-round.

Pass/Permit/Fees: Free access.

Did You Know? The underpass features ever-changing murals painted by local artists, celebrating Santa Barbara's culture and community.

Website:
http://www.santabarbaraca.gov/business/downtown/underpass.asp

SANTA CLARITA

Six Flags Magic Mountain

Unleash your inner thrill-seeker at Six Flags Magic Mountain, a premier amusement park nestled in Valencia, Santa Clarita, California. This adrenaline-packed destination boasts an impressive array of roller coasters, each offering heart-pounding twists and loops that promise an unforgettable ride. You can race on the world-famous Twisted Colossus, soar through the air on Tatsu, or plunge into darkness on X2. The park also features family-friendly rides, live entertainment, and plenty of dining options. With its exhilarating attractions and lively atmosphere, Six Flags Magic Mountain is the ultimate playground for adventure enthusiasts.

Location: 26101 Magic Mountain Pkwy, Valencia, Santa Clarita, CA 91355-1095

Closest City or Town: Santa Clarita, California

How to Get There: From Interstate 5, take the Magic Mountain Parkway exit and follow signs to the park.

GPS Coordinates: 34.4249209° N, 118.5958464° W

Best Time to Visit: Spring and fall for shorter lines and moderate weather.

Pass/Permit/Fees: Admission fees vary; check the website for ticket information.

Did You Know? Six Flags Magic Mountain holds the world record for the most roller coasters in an amusement park, with 19 thrilling rides.

Website: http://www.sixflags.com/magicmountain

SANTA CRUZ

Santa Cruz Beach Boardwalk

Step into the nostalgic charm of the Santa Cruz Beach Boardwalk, a classic seaside amusement park located in Santa Cruz, California. This iconic destination, established in 1907, features a delightful mix of thrilling rides, carnival games, and delectable treats. Take a spin on the historic Giant Dipper roller coaster, enjoy the breathtaking views from the Ferris wheel, and dip your toes in the Pacific Ocean. The vibrant atmosphere, live entertainment, and stunning beach scenery make it a must-visit for families and thrill-seekers alike.

Location: 400 Beach St, Santa Cruz, CA 95060-5416

Closest City or Town: Santa Cruz, California

How to Get There: From Highway 1, take the exit onto Riverside Avenue and follow signs to the boardwalk.

GPS Coordinates: 36.9645218° N, 122.0166672° W

Best Time to Visit: Summer for warm weather and extended operating hours.

Pass/Permit/Fees: Free entry; individual ride tickets and unlimited ride passes are available.

Did You Know? The Santa Cruz Beach Boardwalk's Giant Dipper roller coaster is one of the oldest wooden coasters in the world, operating since 1924.

Website: http://beachboardwalk.com/

SANTA MONICA

Santa Monica Bay

Soak in the sun-drenched beauty of Santa Monica Bay, a picturesque destination located along the Pacific Coast in California. This expansive bay offers miles of sandy beaches, crystal-clear waters, and stunning coastal views. Enjoy a leisurely swim, take a scenic bike ride along the beachfront path, or indulge in the vibrant dining and shopping options nearby. The serene ambiance and diverse recreational opportunities make Santa Monica Bay a perfect spot for relaxation and adventure.

Location: 1550 Pacific Coast Hwy, Santa Monica, CA 90401

Closest City or Town: Santa Monica, California

How to Get There: Accessible via the Pacific Coast Highway; multiple beach access points along the route.

GPS Coordinates: 34.0120753° N, 118.4971221° W

Best Time to Visit: Summer for beach activities and warm weather.

Pass/Permit/Fees: Free access.

Did You Know? Santa Monica Bay is a popular spot for dolphin and whale watching, especially during migration seasons.

Website: https://www.santamonica.gov/

Santa Monica Pier

Experience the quintessential California vibe at the Santa Monica Pier, an iconic landmark perched over the Pacific Ocean in Santa Monica, California. This lively pier offers a mix of amusement park rides, sweet treats, and captivating ocean views. Take a ride on the vintage carousel, enjoy a meal with a view at one of the many restaurants, or cast a line off the pier's end while gazing at the sunset. The Santa Monica Pier, with its historic charm and exciting activities, invites visitors to create lasting memories.

Location: 200 Santa Monica Pier, Santa Monica, CA 90401-3126

Closest City or Town: Santa Monica, California

How to Get There: From Interstate 10, take the 4th Street exit and follow signs to the pier.

GPS Coordinates: 34.0082821° N, 118.4987585° W

Best Time to Visit: Late afternoon to evening for stunning sunset views.

Pass/Permit/Fees: Free access; individual ride tickets available for purchase.

Did You Know? The Santa Monica Pier is home to the Pacific Park amusement park, which features the world's only solar-powered Ferris wheel.

Website: http://santamonicapier.org/

Santa Monica State Beach

Relax on the golden sands of Santa Monica State Beach, a beloved coastal destination located in Santa Monica, California. Stretching for over three miles, this beach offers ample space for sunbathing, swimming, and beach volleyball. You can stroll or bike along the scenic beachfront path, enjoy a picnic with ocean views, or explore the nearby Santa Monica Pier. Its wide sandy shores and inviting waters make it a perfect spot for a day of fun in the sun.

Location: Ocean Ave at Colorado Ave, Santa Monica, CA 90401

Closest City or Town: Santa Monica, California

How to Get There: Accessible from Ocean Avenue, with multiple parking lots along the beach.

GPS Coordinates: 34.0129033° N, 118.5017237° W

Best Time to Visit: Summer for beach activities and warm weather.

Pass/Permit/Fees: Parking fees apply; beach access is free.

Did You Know? Santa Monica State Beach is a prime location for experiencing the iconic California sunsets, often adorned with vibrant hues.

Website: http://www.smgov.net/portals/beach

SANTA ROSA

Safari West

Embark on an African safari adventure without leaving California at Safari West. Nestled in the hills of Santa Rosa, this 400-acre wildlife preserve offers a thrilling opportunity to get up close with giraffes, rhinos, cheetahs, and over 900 other animals. You can join a guided safari tour, stay overnight in luxury tents, and immerse yourself in the sights and sounds of the wild. Unique features include open-air vehicles that take you through expansive savannahs and encounters with rare species. Safari West promises an unforgettable experience of wildlife and wilderness.

Location: 3115 Porter Creek Rd, Santa Rosa, CA 95404-9655

Closest City or Town: Santa Rosa, California

How to Get There: From US-101, take the River Road exit and continue onto Mark West Springs Road, then turn left onto Porter Creek Road.

GPS Coordinates: 38.5569909° N, 122.6961537° W

Best Time to Visit: Spring and fall for mild weather

Pass/Permit/Fees: Tour fees apply; visit the website for details

Did You Know? Safari West is home to endangered species such as the Cape buffalo and the scimitar-horned oryx.

Website: http://www.safariwest.com/

SEQUOIA AND KINGS CANYON NATIONAL PARK

General Sherman Tree

Marvel at the majesty of the General Sherman Tree in Sequoia National Park. This colossal giant sequoia stands as the largest living single-stem tree on Earth, estimated to be around 2,200 years old. You can hike the paved trail that leads to this awe-inspiring natural wonder and stand in its immense shadow, contemplating centuries of history. The park also offers beautiful hiking trails, picnicking spots, and opportunities for serene forest exploration.

Location: 47050 Generals Highway, Sequoia and Kings Canyon National Park, CA 93262

Closest City or Town: Three Rivers, California

How to Get There: From CA-198, navigate to Generals Highway and follow signs for the General Sherman Tree parking area.

GPS Coordinates: 36.5817069° N, 118.7514420° W

Best Time to Visit: Late spring through early fall when trails are clear of snow

Pass/Permit/Fees: National Park entrance fee applies

Did You Know? The General Sherman Tree is about 275 feet tall and has a base circumference of over 100 feet.

Website: https://www.facebook.com/SequoiaKingsNPS/

Moro Rock Trail

Engage in a heart-pounding climb at the Moro Rock Trail in Sequoia National Park. This steep stairway carved into the granite dome provides thrilling ascents and breathtaking views of the surrounding park, including the Kaweah River canyon and Great Western Divide. The trail features 400 steps leading to the summit, where panoramic vistas await. Ideal for adventure seekers, this hike offers both a physical challenge and a visual reward.

Location: Sequoia National Park, Sequoia and Kings Canyon National Park, CA 93262

Closest City or Town: Three Rivers, California

How to Get There: From Generals Highway, follow signs to the Moro Rock parking area, then begin your ascent.

GPS Coordinates: 37.7801637° N, 122.4161985° W

Best Time to Visit: Late spring to early fall for clear weather

Pass/Permit/Fees: National Park entrance fee applies

Did You Know? Moro Rock has been a popular viewing spot since the 1930s, with the steps built by the Civilian Conservation Corps.

Website: http://www.nps.gov/seki/planyourvisit/gfdayhikesum.htm

SIMI VALLEY

Ronald Reagan Presidential Library and Museum

Explore the legacy of a president at the Ronald Reagan Presidential Library and Museum in Simi Valley. This expansive museum covers Ronald Reagan's life, leadership, and contributions to American history. You can tour Air Force One, view presidential artifacts, and even step inside a full-scale replica of the Oval Office. The scenic grounds also offer beautiful gardens and panoramic views of Ventura County, making it both an educational and picturesque visit.

Location: 40 Presidential Dr, Simi Valley, CA 93065-0600

Closest City or Town: Simi Valley, California

How to Get There: From US-101, take the exit for Madera Road and follow signs to Presidential Drive.

GPS Coordinates: 34.2598632° N, 118.8195365° W

Best Time to Visit: Year-round

Pass/Permit/Fees: Admission fees apply; check the website for details

Did You Know? The Reagan Library is home to the final resting place of Ronald and Nancy Reagan.

Website: http://www.reaganlibrary.com/

SOUTH LAKE TAHOE

The Gondola at Heavenly

Experience breathtaking vistas and thrilling heights on The Gondola at Heavenly in South Lake Tahoe. This scenic ride lifts you 2.4 miles up the mountains, offering unmatched views of Lake Tahoe and the Sierra Nevada. At the top, you can explore observation decks, enjoy a range of outdoor activities, or simply soak in the majestic landscape. The gondola operates year-round, providing both winter and summer adventures.

Location: 4080 Lake Tahoe Blvd, The Shops at Heavenly Village, South Lake Tahoe, CA 96150-6907

Closest City or Town: South Lake Tahoe, California

How to Get There: From US-50, drive to Lake Tahoe Blvd and follow signs for The Shops at Heavenly Village.

GPS Coordinates: 38.9561322° N, 119.9429592° W

Best Time to Visit: Year-round, with specific activities available each season

Pass/Permit/Fees: Ticket fees vary; see the website for details

Did You Know? The gondola rises over 3,000 feet, offering views that span two states.

Website: http://www.skiheavenly.com/the-mountain/adventurepeakwinter.aspx

VALLEJO

Six Flags Discovery Kingdom

Unleash your inner thrill-seeker at Six Flags Discovery Kingdom, an exhilarating amusement park in Vallejo, California. This dynamic destination offers a perfect mix of high-flying roller coasters, engaging animal shows, and family-friendly attractions. From the heart-pounding drops of Medusa to the delightful encounters at Dolphin Harbor, there's something for everyone. Unique features include world-class entertainment and the chance to ride some of the most innovative coasters in the nation.

Location: 1001 Fairgrounds Dr, Vallejo, CA 94589-4001

Closest City or Town: Vallejo, California

How to Get There: Located off Interstate 80, take the Fairgrounds Drive exit and follow signs directly to the park.

GPS Coordinates: 38.1376988° N, 122.2334814° W

Best Time to Visit: Spring and Fall for mild weather and fewer crowds

Pass/Permit/Fees: Admission fees vary; seasonal passes and memberships available. Visit the website for details.

Did You Know? Six Flags Discovery Kingdom is the only Six Flags park in California with a combination of marine and land animal attractions.

Website: https://www.sixflags.com/discoverykingdom

YERMO

Calico Ghost Town

Step back in time at Calico Ghost Town, a beautifully preserved mining town in Yermo, California. Once a booming silver mining town in the 1880s, it now offers visitors a nostalgic journey through history. Explore old mine shafts, browse historic buildings, and enjoy engaging reenactments of Wild West life. The town's unique charm lies in its authenticity, providing a genuine taste of the Old West.

Location: 36600 Ghost Town Rd, Yermo, CA 92398-0406

Closest City or Town: Yermo, California

How to Get There: From Interstate 15, take the Ghost Town Road exit and follow signs to the town entrance.

GPS Coordinates: 34.9509908° N, 116.8651899° W

Best Time to Visit: Fall and Spring for pleasant weather

Pass/Permit/Fees: Admission fees apply; visit the website for more details.

Did You Know? Calico Ghost Town is a California Historical Landmark, reflecting its important contribution to the state's mining history.

Website: http://www.calicotown.com/

YOSEMITE NATIONAL PARK

Glacier Point

Marvel at the breathtaking vistas from Glacier Point, a stunning viewpoint in Yosemite Valley, California. Perched high above the valley floor, this iconic spot offers panoramic views of Half Dome, Yosemite Falls, and the vast wilderness below. Visitors can enjoy hiking trails, photography opportunities, and serene moments surrounded by nature's grandeur. Unique features include its accessibility for all and the unparalleled views that capture Yosemite's essence.

Location: PCHG+8H Yosemite Valley, California

Closest City or Town: Yosemite Valley, California

How to Get There: Accessible via Glacier Point Road from Wawona Road (Highway 41). Follow signs within Yosemite National Park.

GPS Coordinates: 37.6738854° N, 119.6381353° W

Best Time to Visit: Late Spring through Early Fall when the road is open

Pass/Permit/Fees: Entrance fee required for Yosemite National Park; no additional fee for Glacier Point

Did You Know? Glacier Point provides a view that's equivalent to looking down from a 3,200-foot tall cliff, offering some of the park's best scenery.

Website: http://www.nps.gov/yose/planyourvisit/glacierpoint.htm/

Mariposa Grove of Giant Sequoias

Feel the awe as you wander through Mariposa Grove of Giant Sequoias in Yosemite National Park, California. Home to some of the world's largest and oldest trees, these majestic sequoias stand as silent witnesses to thousands of years. Visitors can hike serene trails, marvel at the towering Grizzly Giant, and reflect on nature's grandeur. This grove's unique charm lies in its combination of accessibility and ancient beauty.

Location: Mariposa Grove Road, Yosemite National Park, CA 95389

Closest City or Town: Yosemite National Park, California

How to Get There: From South Entrance on Highway 41, take Mariposa Grove Road to the parking area and follow signs for shuttle service.

GPS Coordinates: 37.5135960° N, 119.5968160° W

Best Time to Visit: Spring through Fall for ideal trail conditions

Pass/Permit/Fees: Entrance fee required for Yosemite National Park; free shuttle service to the grove.

Did You Know? The Mariposa Grove is home to over 500 giant sequoias, some as old as 3,000 years.

Website: http://www.nps.gov/yose/planyourvisit/mg.htm

Tunnel View

Marvel at the iconic scenery from Tunnel View, one of Yosemite National Park's most celebrated vistas. Located on Wawona Road, this viewpoint offers breathtaking panoramas of Yosemite Valley, El Capitan, Half Dome, and Bridalveil Fall. You can capture stunning photographs, enjoy a serene picnic, or simply stand in awe of nature's grandeur. This spot is perfect for anyone looking to witness the awe-inspiring beauty that makes Yosemite a global treasure.

Location: Wawona Road, Yosemite National Park, CA 95389

Closest City or Town: Yosemite Valley, California

How to Get There: From Wawona Road (Highway 41), follow signs to Tunnel View just east of the Wawona Tunnel.

GPS Coordinates: 37.7157987° N, 119.6774827° W

Best Time to Visit: Year-round, with clear days offering the best visibility.

Pass/Permit/Fees: Entrance fee required for Yosemite National Park.

Did You Know? Tunnel View was constructed in 1933 and has since become one of the most photographed spots in Yosemite.

Website: http://www.nps.gov/yose/naturescience/scenic-vistas-tunnel-view.htm

Yosemite Falls

Feel the power of nature at Yosemite Falls, North America's tallest waterfall, cascading a dramatic 2,425 feet. Located in Yosemite Valley, this natural wonder comprises three sections: Upper Falls, Middle Cascades, and Lower Falls. You can hike the short Lower Falls trail for an up-close view, or embark on the more challenging trail to the top of Upper Falls. Witnessing Yosemite Falls in full flow, especially during spring runoff, offers an unforgettable experience for nature enthusiasts.

Location: QC43+J6 Yosemite Valley, California

Closest City or Town: Yosemite Valley, California

How to Get There: From Yosemite Valley, take Northside Drive or Southside Drive to the Yosemite Falls parking area, and follow signs to the falls.

GPS Coordinates: 37.7565957° N, 119.5969074° W

Best Time to Visit: Spring to early summer, when the waterfall is at its most powerful.

Pass/Permit/Fees: Entrance fee required for Yosemite National Park.

Did You Know? Yosemite Falls is so tall that gusts of wind can evaporate parts of the waterfall before they reach the ground.

Website:
http://www.nps.gov/yose/planyourvisit/yosemitefallstrail.htm

MAP

We have devised an interactive map that includes all destinations described in the book.

Upon scanning a provided QR code, a link will be sent to your email, allowing you access to this unique digital feature.

This map is both detailed and user-friendly, marking every location described within the pages of the book. It provides accurate addresses and GPS coordinates for each location, coupled with direct links to the websites of these stunning destinations.

Once you receive your email link and access the interactive map, you'll have an immediate and comprehensive overview of each site's location. This invaluable tool simplifies trip planning and navigation, making it a crucial asset for both first-time visitors and seasoned explorers of Washington.

Scan the following QR or type in the provided link to receive it:

https://jo.my/californiabucketlistbonus

You will receive an email with links to access the Interactive Map. If you do not see our email, please look for it in spam or another section of your inbox.

In case you have any problems, you can write us at
TravelBucketList@becrepress.com

Made in the USA
Las Vegas, NV
16 December 2024

14479018R00066